Timing the *San Diego* Real Estate Market

The Campbell Method:
A Proven System for Buying and Selling
Real Estate for Maximum Profits

Third Edition

Robert M. Campbell

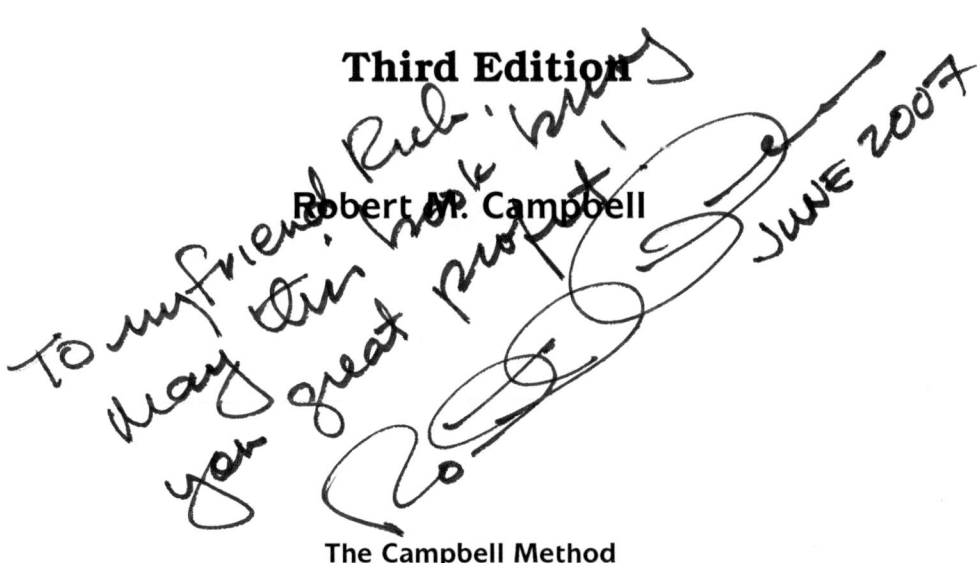

The Campbell Method
San Diego, California

Timing The San Diego Real Estate Market

Copyright © 2002, 2004, 2007 by Robert M. Campbell

All rights reserved. No part of this book may be reproduced or distributed in any form or by any means, electronic or mechanical, including photocopying, recording by any information storage or retrieval system — without written permission from the publisher, except for the inclusion of brief quotations in a review.

For information, please contact The Campbell Method, 3525 Del Mar Heights Road, #634, San Diego, CA 92130. Discounts for bulk orders are available.

"The Campbell Method" is a pending trademark.

ISBN: 0-9724418-1-6

Third Edition: January 2007

Dedication

To the millions of home buyers and home sellers who — every year — regretfully say:

"If I had only bought (or sold) a year or two earlier . . .

I would have made a killing."

May this book help show you the light.

Contents

Warning — Disclaimer vii

Introduction 9

Chapter 1 17
 Cycles of Boom and Bust

Chapter 2 31
 Forget "Location, Location, Location" . . .
 It's All About Timing

Chapter 3 41
 The Great Real Estate Discovery

Chapter 4 53
 The Five Vital Signs Indicators:
 Your Window into the Future

Chapter 5 63
 The World's First Billionaire Shares His Secret

Chapter 6 71
 Calculating Vital Sign Trends:
 Don't Sweat The Math

Chapter 7 87
 The Best Time to Buy:
 A Vital Signs Case Study

Chapter 8 99
    The Best Time to Sell:
    A Vital Signs Case Study

Chapter 9 111
    The Campbell Method:
    Three Market Truths

Chapter 10 117
    The Campbell Method:
    A Timing System With Ten Cardinal Rules

Chapter 11 127
    Putting It All Together:
    Trends Never End, They Only Change Directions

Chapter 12 135
    Final Words:
    A Real Estate Breakthrough

Appendix 137

About The Author 185

Warning — Disclaimer

This publication is intended to provide accurate and authoritative information with regard to the subject matter covered. It is offered with the understanding that neither the publisher nor the author is engaged in rendering legal, tax or other professional services. If legal, tax or other expert assistance is required, the services of a competent professional should be sought.

It is not the purpose of this book to give you all the information you need or that is available to make the most profitable decisions. You are urged to read all the material available, learn as much as possible about real estate, and tailor the information in this book to your own individual needs and circumstances.

Investing in real estate is not a get-rich-quick scheme nor is there any guarantee that you will make a profit. You can lose money in real estate; readers, therefore, are advised to proceed with caution with respect to the techniques described in this book. Anyone who decides to invest for a profit must expect to put a lot of time and effort into it, and there are still no guarantees that you will be successful.

Every effort has been made to make this book as complete and accurate as possible. However, there may be mistakes, both typographical and in content. Therefore, this book should be used only as a general guide and not as the ultimate source for making money in real estate. Information contained herein has been carefully gathered from sources believed to be reliable but cannot be guaranteed as to its accuracy or completeness.

The purpose of this book is to educate and entertain. The author and publisher shall have neither liability nor responsibility to any person or entity with respect to any loss or damage caused, or alleged to have been caused, directly or indirectly, by the information contained in this book. There is no guarantee that any recommendations, strategies, or methods used in this book will be profitable or that past performance is a guarantee of future results. Those using this information are responsible for their own actions.

If you do not wish to be bound by the above, you may return this book to the publisher anytime within 30 days of purchase for a full refund.

Introduction

*To swim a fast 100 meters, it's better to swim
with the tide than to work on your stroke.*
— Warren Buffett

When it comes to making money in real estate, nothing beats good timing.

When you buy or sell a home, anything you can do to improve your timing is like money in the bank. Yes, timing is everything. In all aspects of life, especially real estate, this is a simple and obvious truth.

Timing the San Diego Real Estate Market offers you a revolutionary approach to making money in real estate, one that focuses on fast growth of capital and low risk. Based on 30-years experience as a real estate broker and investor, and a keen interest in finding ways to stay ahead of market trends, Robert Campbell has developed a logical, market-proven, and clearly-defined approach — *The Campbell Method* — that shows you how to anticipate *residential* real estate trends so that you can make intelligent and informed decisions about when to buy and sell.

The Campbell Method asks you to look at the market objectively, not emotionally. It requires that you step away from your own personal beliefs, opinions and biases about what you would *like* the market to do, and focus instead on what the market is telling you to do. Here is what *The Campbell Method* will help you identify to capture the greatest real estate profits:

- Five key Vital Sign indicators that track the trend of the real estate market.

- Three Market Truths that teach you to respect what the market is telling you to do.

- Ten Cardinal Rules that tell you what to do and when to do it.

Whether you are a homeowner or an investor, a savvy veteran or someone who is just starting out in real estate, using *The Campbell Method* to buy and sell will give you a tremendous advantage over those who play the guessing game.

Your awareness of what is happening in the real estate market will vastly expand.

You will see trends more clearly. It will become easier to anticipate the future direction of the market.

You will be more relaxed and confident — and less nervous and uncertain — when it comes to making important decisions that can cost you money if you are wrong. Because you will be plugged into the flow of the market, you will know when to take action and when to sit tight.

You will make more money in real estate. It will become easier to break away from buying and selling habits that may have yielded only limited success in the past.

The Law of Real Estate Markets

Everyone knows there is a natural, irrefutable law to all markets: *prices rise and prices fall*. Real estate is no exception. The pendulum swings back and forth from good markets to bad markets, building wealth and then tearing it down.

Even though estimates vary widely from one geographic region to another, on a national basis, the prevailing economic view seems to be that home prices rise an average of 40-60% during the market uptrends and then fall an average of 20-30% during the downtrends. In other words, two steps forward and one step back. In Southern California, where the market research for this book was conducted, these price swings have been even more extreme.

With such dramatic price movement in home values, it is no surprise that the trends can make you rich from real estate ownership; however, the same trends can also make you poor. While risk and reward are always present in the marketplace, it is important to learn how to stack the odds decidedly in your favor.

It's Not What You Do . . . But When You Do It

Have you ever tried to grow crops in the *wintertime*? You have to spend days or weeks preparing the soil, use special fertilizers to stimulate growth, and then find ways to protect the seedlings from the elements. Even after all this hard work, the crops still struggle to survive . . . and most die.

On the other hand, if you wait until *springtime* to grow crops, it is a totally different story. All you have to do it take handfuls of seeds and toss them on the ground, and without doing much of anything . . . Presto! They grow like crazy.

Then, during the *summertime*, the crops become fully grown and your efforts produce the highest possible yield. This is when it is time to harvest and collect the full benefits of your labors. However, if you wait too long to harvest, the crops will start to wither, and then eventually die. In other words, the greater the delay, the greater the risk of loss.

This good timing, bad timing principle works exactly the same way in real estate.

When you buy real estate at the right time — when prices are at a market cycle low — and sell real estate at the right time — when prices are at a market cycle high — you can make optimal returns with minimal risk.

The lesson is simple: whether you are growing crops for the greatest yield, or buying and selling real estate for the greatest profits, *there is a time to sow and a time to reap.*

The Coming Economic Upheavals: When to Buy

While some forecasters believe the future is bright, and others believe another depression is right around the corner, no one has a crystal ball that can see into the future.

Whatever your personal viewpoint about what lies ahead — whether you are an optimist or a pessimist — one thing *is* certain: change is unavoidable. Cycles of boom and bust are as predictable as the changing seasons and the tides. While the course of mankind is ever upward, there will always be major setbacks — and major real estate downturns — along the way.

History does repeat. If you live to be 75 years old and regardless where you live in the United States, chances are good that you will experience one *serious recession* every ten years, and one *economic depression* at some point in your lifetime. While "New Era" promises of lasting prosperity come and go, there is no reason to expect that this reoccurring pattern will not continue.

What is ironic, however, is that while the long-term trend of real estate prices continues to ratchet higher, it is the market downturns that ultimately offer you the greatest opportunity to profit. In fact, when you buy at a market cycle bottom (just before the market turns up again), this will likely be the easiest money you will ever make in real estate. This is because there are always plenty of screaming bargains available from highly motivated and even desperate sellers, who unfortunately find themselves in trouble.

The Campbell Method teaches you how to pinpoint when the market has hit bottom and is ready to climb higher, so that you can take advantage of these tremendous real estate bargains.

When to Sell

Mistakenly, most people believe real estate is always a safe investment. Although you can make spectacular profits *with low risk* during rising markets, nothing goes up forever. Sooner or later rising markets turn into falling markets. When this happens, when real estate values go into major decline (even if its not as bad as the 1929 crash), some or all of your profits can be quickly wiped out in what seems like the blink of an eye.

To protect your real estate profits, you have to know when to sell.

In fact, knowing when to sell is even more important than knowing when to buy. Why? Because the loss of *real* profits always takes priority over missing out on *potential* profits. After all, there will always be new real estate trends to catch. But if you lose your money because of bad timing, you may not be in position to grab the brass ring when the next market cycle hits bottom again.

If you invest in real estate wisely — knowing that when to sell is key — your alertness can protect you from problems that may seriously hurt or break others. It is easy to see how "selling high" also puts you in the ideal cash position to "buy low" after prices fall.

Whether the future holds good times or bad times for the real estate market, *The Campbell Method* prepares you for both.

Timing the Market for Maximum Profits

While housing markets vary greatly by region, historically, real estate trends tend to last about three to five years on the upside and three to five years on the downside. To really profit during the good markets and, more importantly, protect your profits from the bad markets, you must be able to *anticipate* these trend reversals.

To do this, you have to look *deeper into market events* than what is reported on headline news or what is held true by mass thinking. These approaches put you behind the curve, not ahead of it.

So, how can you *anticipate* when these trend changes are coming? How can you tell when the market will boom . . . and when it will crash?

The Campbell Method for timing the real estate market shows you how to track the trend of the market by using five key real estate indicators called "Vital Signs." These market bell weathers are "leading indicators" to what is on the horizon for real estate prices and will give you a three to six month "window into the future." This *early warning detection system* gives you the strategic advantage of being able to buy and sell *before* mass crowd psychology starts to move real estate prices higher or lower in a significant way.

What the Vital Sign Indicators Tell You

The Vital Sign indicators directly measure supply and demand pressures that are building in the real estate market. By letting the market disclose what it is going to do next, you can rely on these indicators to tell you:

- When home prices are approaching a market peak.
- When home prices are approaching a market bottom.
- When home prices are in market uptrends or downtrends.

Clearly, the better you can anticipate real estate trends, the more likely you are to profit. Wayne Gretzky, the greatest hockey player to ever play the game, put it this way:

"Go where the puck is headed, not where it is."

Knowing how to use the information that these Vital Sign indicators provide can produce staggering results. Imagine the profits you could achieve if you were able to anticipate the "high" and "low" points of the real estate cycle three to six months ahead of the general public? It would be like winning the lottery!

Why ride the market cycle up and then ride it back down? The key is to buy at the bottom and sell at the top. If you like roller coaster rides, go to the amusement park.

Big Mistakes in Real Estate and How to Avoid Them

Buying near market cycle bottoms can make you rich and *buying near market cycle peaks can make you poor.* The reason for this is simple: if you buy a home at a highly inflated price, you stand to lose much more than you make. Remember, since there is no protective moat built around real estate values, what may appear to be the American Dream can quickly turn into a nightmare if you are not careful. Home prices — especially in California and other high priced housing markets — can drop up to 30% or more during market declines.

When you buy at a market peak, a $250,000 home will drop in value to $175,000 during a 30% market decline. This means the same home would have to appreciate by a whopping 43% *just to break even.* Even though home prices have steadily risen since the 1950's, waiting years and years to "get even" is hardly a good way to make money in real estate or get ahead in life.

The risk of "buying high" at market peaks becomes even more perilous when you consider how downturns in the economy closely parallel downturns in the real estate market. For better or worse, 15-20% of the economy is directly linked to the health of the real estate business. It is called the "wealth effect." Therefore, if you "buy high," it is likely you will be over-burdened with a big mortgage (debt) on a home that is sinking in value. Then, as the economy unravels—this is especially true if you lose your job, your savings, or your home — the negative effects on you and your family can be devastating.

Maximum Profits with Minimum Risk

The Campbell Method for timing the real estate market shows you a *safe* and *rewarding* way to buy and sell real estate. Using market insights generated by the Vital Sign calculations, you will know to buy before the market starts to move up . . . and to sell before the market starts to move down.

Simply put, as the Vital Sign indicators go . . . so goes the real estate market.

Realize this: real estate trends never end. Sooner or later — good or bad — these trends only change direction. If you stay alert and prepare yourself for these approaching trend changes, you can place yourself in the *extreme minority of people* who will prosper from whatever direction the real estate market (and the economy) moves.

The Campbell Method is not a gimmick or a get-rich-overnight scheme. It is a fresh new approach to buying and selling real estate that shows you how to maximize profits and minimize risk by intelligently moving money into and out of the market, not by whim, but by careful, well thought out analysis of trends. When you master the market timing skills presented in this book, your success in real estate will be secure.

There is an old saying in the markets: "Nobody rings a bell when the market peaks or hits bottom." But contrary to common belief, when you apply *The Campbell Method* for *Timing the San Diego Real Estate Market*, that bell can ring for you.

– Chapter 1 –

Cycles of Boom and Bust

Those who cannot remember the past are doomed to repeat it.
— George Santayana

A million years ago, the caveman made an important discovery about how to adjust to the world around him. Seeing that summer and winter repeated on regular intervals, he learned that storing food and fuel during the warm and plentiful times of summer allowed him to survive the lean and cold times of winter.

Just like the caveman learned how to identify a simple summer-to-winter cycle, it is possible to identify similar cycles in the real estate market.

The Campbell Method for timing the real estate market offers compelling proof that it is possible. Like the tides, the moon, and the seasons, real estate markets also have their cycles. These cycles are simply natural fluctuations in market activity—alternating between periods of rising and falling prices. Even though real estate cycles will always have an element of mystery, and are not as regular as the cycles of nature, there is no law that states that they have to catch you off-guard.

Real estate cycles go through *stages* that are logical, understandable, explainable, and can be identified by the Vital Sign indicators. However, before you learn about these indicators, it is important for you to first develop a clear awareness of the nature of market psychology and the telltale characteristics that identify when one market cycle stage is coming to an end . . . and another is just beginning.

It is easy to see why "stage identification" is critically important for making money in real estate. Timing, and how well you do, all starts with the stage in which you buy. Of course, buying in the early stages of a rising market will yield the greatest profits. Buying in the middle stages of a real estate upcycle will also be profitable, but it will not result in the huge payoff made from buying in the early stage. You should also keep in mind that buying in the late stages of a market upcycle is dangerous; it increases your risk and decreases your odds of success. In fact, this is the time you should be thinking about selling (to protect profits), and not buying into an inflated and overpriced market.

Why Real Estate Moves Up and Down in Cycles

While people who buy and sell real estate are all distinctly different, as a collective group you can count on them to share the same predictable tendencies. And it is this unifying factor we call "human nature" that sets real estate trends in motion and can take the market from boom to bust . . . and then back to boom all over again.

The first thing to recognize is that people generally have a tendency, and this is especially true in real estate, to "follow the crowd." Driven by alternating periods of greed and fear, or of optimism and pessimism, or of ecstasy and despair, the human animal can be counted on to march to a predictable drumbeat. This herd mentality is a big reason why real estate prices rise — and fall — in alternating periods of over-and under-valuation.

Secondly, people tend to hold onto the belief that whatever the existing trend is, that trend will continue to operate in the future. This phenomenon is most evident at the peaks and valleys of the real estate cycle, where everybody wants to buy real estate when it is expensive yet nobody wants it when it is cheap.

This being the case, understanding human nature can help you make more profitable buying and selling decisions. It will allow you to overcome your own self-defeating tendencies by becoming a more flexible and independent thinker. Then, once you can see the market as it really is — and not be held prisoner by the follow-the-leader mentality of the crowd — you will be able to be constantly thinking about change and the best way to deal with it. Last but not least, you will then be able to identify the market's direction and anticipate its next move. In other words, you will be able to tell when real estate is at a market cycle bottom and when it is at a market cycle peak.

The truth is, *great real estate investors are made, not born.* What is required is discipline, a system that tells you when to buy — not what to buy — and a strategic plan for moving money in and out of the market. And contrary to popular belief, what is *not required* is superior intelligence. Even the brightest person will lose money if he buys near a market cycle peak and the market heads south. On the other hand, a real estate novice will make money if he or she buys near the bottom and rides the market cycle up.

Although we would all like to act on "inside information," and know the true "scoop" on what is going to happen before everyone else, the skilled observer who has *learned* where to look, has the best possible chance to know in advance where and when each stage of the real estate cycle is approaching.

Real estate cycles go through four distinct stages that are predictable patterns of change:

Stage One: The bottom of a market cycle, when real estate is a bargain.

Stage Two: Prices start to climb. People notice this, which creates a demand that keeps prices rising until the demand slows, at which point real estate becomes over-priced.

Stage Three: Prices hit a peak and level off.

Stage Chart

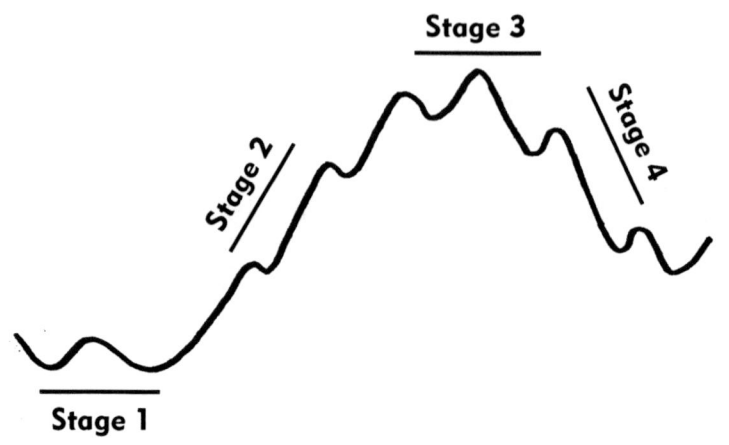

Chart 1-1: The Four Stages of a Real Estate Cycle

Stage Four: Prices begin to fall. As prices begin to drop, people hold off from buying until real estate becomes under-priced and is a bargain again.

Then the cycle repeats itself.

Studies show that as real estate prices move from one stage to another stage, so does market psychology. What this means is that psychological change is the engine of the market and that most people's buying and selling decisions are basically driven by two powerful emotions, fear and greed. Fear and greed, however, are poor financial advisors. Greed, for example, typically leads you into buying at or near real estate peaks, the times when you should be selling. What is just as bad is that fear makes you give up all hope at market bottoms, the time when you should be buying.

If we look at a complete real estate cycle, we will see that each full cycle goes through identifiable periods of growth, maturity, and decay, which will be followed by a re-emergence of growth that starts a new market cycle all over again. It is important to understand that all real estate cycles are self-perpetuating. In other words, one cycle fuels the next.

As property values rise higher and higher (during the growth phase), the seeds of self-destruction are already building in the upcycle. This is because rising prices eventually reach a high point that curtails buyer demand. Conversely, as property values fall lower and lower (during the decay phase), the seeds of regeneration are building in the downcycle. Because falling home prices eventually reach a low point where there is an abundance of interested buyers, but few sellers, prices have nowhere to go but up. For these reasons, all real estate cycles push home prices only so high — or so low — before they reverse direction.

Stage One:
The Market Hits Rock-Bottom

Stage One is the market bottom. During this time real estate prices are depressed, often severely. Current business news is usually terrible. Market analysts tend to be equally pessimistic. A large percentage of real estate offices have closed, and up to 50% of all real estate agents may have left the business. Everywhere you go, you hear about those who are losing their shirts in the real estate market and the many homebuilders who are in trouble or now bankrupt.

At *Stage One*, everyone who has been scared or forced into selling has sold. There are few buyers and few sellers . . . yet equilibrium between supply and demand has been reached. Prices are unlikely to fall much lower. Property is cheap and bargains are everywhere, yet very few have the foresight, or the courage, to step in and buy. Value is ignored. Blinded by fear and uncertainty, buyers are looking into the rear-view mirror to see what prices have done in the recent past, instead of looking through the windshield to see where prices are likely to go in the near future.

On the other side of the coin, those buyers who take advantage of this low risk buying opportunity are the ones who make the greatest profits. To illustrate, let me tell you about a new home I bought in early 1982, which was a time when the San Diego real estate market was depressed and still reeling both from recession and the negative effect of the 17% mortgage rates from the previous year.

Buying from a "highly motivated" homebuilder at the *low price* of $205,000 — remember, we are talking about San Diego here — my timing proved to be perfect! (Even though my Vital Sign indicators were not discovered until 1993, market research — i.e. "back-testing" — shows these key indicators signaled a *Stage One* market cycle bottom for the San Diego real estate in April 1982.) As luck would have it, the value of the home started to rise as soon as I closed escrow. A mere six years later (Spring 1988), I sold the home for $375,000, which constituted an 83% appreciation in value. This amounted to a profit of $170,000, a staggering 829% return on my initial $20,500 down payment!

Stage Two:
The Market Blastoff and Uptrend

Stage Two begins when real estate prices slowly start to rise. As time goes by, people begin to notice that prices are moving higher, and become more interested in buying. This signals that the start of a new market cycle uptrend is underway. It is during this stage that you want to have your money invested in real estate. The earlier you buy, the better. As demand rises, higher prices are bound to follow.

As more time passes during *Stage Two*, and as prices continue to rise, the pain of the last market downtrend starts to fade from memory. Buyers who have been waiting on the sidelines now start jumping into the market, little by little pushing prices even higher. Increasing property values attract more and more people who are eager to buy, which drives prices higher still. Like a self-fulfilling prophecy, steadily increasing demand fuels a rising real estate market that starts to feed upon itself.

This is the growth stage for real estate values.

After a year or so of rising prices, as more and more buyers stampede into the market, prices continue to surge higher and higher. Demand continues to build. And as prices go even higher — and property values start to rise at a faster and faster clip — we see an emergence of speculators entering the market for one purpose only: to make a rapid profit.

In 1984, for example, with the San Diego real estate market appreciating by almost ten percent, I personally started investing in real estate in a more speculative way. That is, instead of buying "existing properties" for investment — like I had always done since 1972 — I decided to go into real estate development in order to speed up the wealth building process. So, with the San Diego real estate market in a *Stage Two* uptrend until late 1989, I followed in my father's footsteps as a builder, and from 1984 to 1988, I successful built — and sold — over 40 homes and apartment units. With the "trend as my friend," my net worth went into a steep upward climb and the champagne corks were popping!

The point of telling you this story is to underline the fact that, in the middle of a *Stage Two* market upcycle, when property values can start to climb at double-digit rates of appreciation, rising real estate prices eventually start to make headline news. Typically, this is when the general public starts to exhibit more and more buying interest. As they buy in greater and greater numbers, prices are pushed even higher. The ranks of real estate agents swell to handle the increased demand. Now the social buzz becomes one of excitement, and everybody is talking about how people are making a "killing" in real estate.

As the market continues to boom late into the *Stage Two* upcycle, the economists and real estate "experts" are all uniformly optimistic in their economic outlooks. Now, even the real estate skeptics who had been content to watch from the sidelines up to this point become convinced it is time to join the party. So they jump on the bandwagon in huge numbers and rush into the market to buy, often engaging in overbidding wars to make sure that they won't be priced out of the market forever. "Home prices may be high," they rationalize, "but they are going even higher."

The longer the *Stage Two* uptrend continues, the more the growing risk that is lurking around the corner is ignored even after prices reach ridiculous levels. And when the big run-up in real estate prices sets off the alarm bells, very few are willing to listen.

Unfortunately, it always turns out that what the wise do early, the foolish do late. The growth phase of the real estate cycle is about to come to a screeching halt, and money invested in real estate is now potentially at great risk.

Stage Three:
The Market Hits a Peak

Stage Three arrives when real estate prices reach a market cycle peak and start to level off. Most people who were interested in buying, have done so. Real estate is now overpriced.

The "Greater Fool Theory," which presumes that you can pay any absurd price for a property, and there will be someone greedier than you who will buy it from you at an even higher price, has been pushed to its limit.

With fewer and fewer buyers willing — or able — to pay these highly inflated prices, demand starts to slow. Oddly enough, even though the upward trend in real estate prices has stalled, there are still enthusiasts who believe prices will soon be moving higher again in the near future. They like to cite "facts" that prove there is an absolute shortage of housing that will permanently support prices at these absurd levels.

As more and more time passes with little or no price appreciation (there is no place left to go), the best informed begin to recognize this is a real estate "peak." This is when market risk is highest. With sluggish demand, a few sellers reluctantly start to lower their asking prices — usually to "market value" — to attract buyers. The buyers who jump in do so with the confidence that they are making a "good buy." While the momentum of the mar-ket's upcycle may indeed cause prices to rise for a little while longer, this is the beginning of the end. Soon, the buyers who thought they were making a good buy will be kissing their money "good-bye."

Those who sell at the end of *Stage Three* — by design or sheer luck — will be selling at high prices that are unlikely to be seen for years to come. Those who overstay their welcome do so at extreme peril.

Stage Four:
The Downturn and Possible Market Crash

Stage Four begins when real estate prices start to fall. This signals that the market is now turning downward, and it is during this stage that you want to have your money out of the real estate market. Sales activity starts to slow because there are fewer buyers. When prices first start to fall, there is disbelief and denial from sellers, just like the denial and disbelief you will hear from buyers at the start of the *Stage Two* market uptrend.

"Real estate prices will go back up soon," plead the real estate agents, who are now all looking for ways to boost their disappearing sales.

During market downturns, sellers and real estate listing agents start to use incentives to lure buyers. One common tactic is to offer a large "selling bonus" (higher commission) to agents who have buyers who still believe real estate is a safe investment. Homebuilders use even a wider assortment of incentives to stimulate sales. They try to "bribe" buyers with free landscaping, new cars, vacations, and almost anything else you can imagine.

Personally, I liked to use "creative financing" as a way to attract buyers during a *Stage Four* market downcycle. In 1980, for example, with mortgage rates at 13% and rising, a highly inflated San Diego real estate market finally started to deflate. I owned about eight to ten rental properties at that time, and many of my real estate brokerage clients were investing as well. Because our rentals were all highly leveraged in order to "max-out" our returns during the late 1970's upcycle, most of our properties had a negative cash flow, meaning the rental income did not cover the holding costs.

With San Diego real estate prices now dropping each month (along with the cash reserves in our bank accounts), my clients and I knew we had to act fast. To solve the problem, we sold nine or ten rental properties within two to three months with "no money down" and "no new bank financing" required, a strategy which is the essence of creative financing. By doing this, we were able to sell quickly at high prices, eliminate negative cash flows, and protect our "paper profits."

After one or two years into a *Stage Four* decline, demand continues to slow and the reality of falling prices becomes increasingly obvious. To many, the unthinkable is now unfolding: real estate can actually go down in value. Prices may be lower by 10-20% from the previous peak. While most sellers have given up hope of making a profit, many are adamant about not taking a loss. They try to sell their homes for exactly what they paid. However, unless the price of a property has been "marked down" sufficiently to be attractive to a dwindling pool of buyers, the amount of loss continues to grow.

Errors in market timing become particularly heightened when illiquid investors are caught holding real estate that produces negative cash flows. These types of properties are known as "alligators." If prices don't appreciate as expected, what happens is the monthly bleed causes investors to run out of cash to feed these alligators and the roof caves in. Simply put, if you guess wrong about the direction of the market while owning negative cash flow properties, you will soon be tossed from the marketplace with the same care and compassion that a barroom bouncer gives a drunken patron.

If the real estate market goes into a severe decline, home prices can fall by 20-30%, or more. The value of vacant land really gets smashed; it can drop by 50%, as I know from personal experience. After my partners and I bought two multi-family building sites — one for $600,000 and another for $370,000 — at the peak of the San Diego real estate boom in 1989, the market crashed. By 1992, both pieces of land were sold for their loan amounts. With the complete loss of our down payments, plus three years of $6000-per-month holding costs, the total loss was nearly $600,000. (It was this financial disaster — plus another caused by my decision to build an eight-home subdivision at the same time — that led to the discovery of the Vital Sign indicators.)

When the market gets really bad, sales activity slows to a crawl. Real estate agents are now exiting the business in droves. A market that was once driven by greed is now driven by fear. The local economy is depressed and unemployment is high. With layoffs getting worse, an increasing number of property owners are now having trouble making their mortgage payments. In desperation, they phone their real estate agents and say, "I need to sell my home immediately." Some agents reply, "Sell to whom? There aren't any buyers."

Other property owners don't want to make their mortgage payments because they've become what is known as "upside-down," meaning that they owe more on their homes than their homes are worth. Whatever the reason, the result is the same:

Source: *North County Times, San Diego, CA* **November 14, 1993**

foreclosures skyrocket, putting even more downward pressure on already depressed prices.

At the end of a Stage Four decline, when despair is most rampant, the market eventually finds a bottom. After the huge fall in real estate prices, the bells start ringing again . . . this time as a major opportunity to buy.

The dark skies begin to clear and the sun begins to shine again, signaling the dawn of a new market cycle uptrend . . . If you have the knowledge to recognize this as a market bottom, have money and the courage to act, you are now in the perfect position to make the buys of a lifetime.

Real Estate Cycles Play a Vital Role in Your Life

Know this: even though the population continues to grow and there are more and more governmental programs — called "safety nets" — in place to prevent serious downturns in our economy (at least in theory), real estate cycles will always exist. The forces of supply and demand are so powerful, and shifts in market sentiment from optimism to pessimism are so strong, that even government action cannot prevent periods when property values fall.

Both from a study of history as well as this author's personal experiences, what the market gives, the market can also take away. For this reason, when you buy a home–and when you sell it — real estate timing will be central if your goal is to increase your wealth.

Because of the long-term nature of real estate ownership, for many it is difficult to grasp the true potential of buying and selling according to market cycles. For others, especially the inexperienced with dollar signs dancing in their eyes, the expectation often exists that real estate is the place to make a spectacular killing regardless of when they buy in the cycle. Either way, this lack of market cycle awareness not only limits profits, but it also creates unnecessary exposure to risk.

Knowing that real estate cycles exist, however, is not enough. To take advantage of them, you must know how to anticipate their arrival.

The Best Time to Buy and Sell? Just Ask the Market

Real estate cycles — and trends — don't just happen by accident. They are not random events that occur for no reason. Instead, they are set in motion by a series of economic events that create supply and demand imbalances in the marketplace, circumstances which can be directly measured by the Vital Sign indicators.

The Vital Sign indicators prove that in order to stay ahead of these trends, you don't have to be the smartest person in the world. You don't have to figure out what the baby boomers are going to do about housing, whether inflation is going to get better or worse, or how the war on terrorism is ultimately going to impact the economy. While all these topics may make for interesting discussions at your local Starbucks, you don't need to know these answers to make intelligent real estate decisions.

Furthermore, even *if* you could answer these kinds of questions, it still may not be enough. The reason for this is that real estate trends are influenced by a whole host of market forces — interest rates, the expansion or contraction of the economy, consumer confidence, income levels, inflation, population trends, changes in the tax laws, and even war. To complicate matters even more and add to the confusion, at any point in time, some of these market forces are exerting a positive effect on real estate prices while others are exerting a negative effect.

So, how can you figure out what real estate prices are going to do next?

There is only one answer, and if you want to know for sure, the market itself has it.

– Chapter 2 –

Forget "Location, Location, Location" . . . It's All About Timing!

In selecting the soundest financial investments, the question of when to buy is far more important than what to buy.
— Roger W. Babson

Every decade or so, the real estate market in every American city reaches two major turning points. The first occurs at *Stage One* market cycle bottoms, when real estate prices are cheap, where you are provided the opportunity to buy into the American dream: the single-family home, at a bargain price. The second occurs years later at *Stage Three* market cycle peaks, when you will come face-to-face with another wonderful opportunity. It is here that you will have the chance to sell your home for way more than you paid for it — often at an unthinkably high price.

Make no mistake about it, *change* (price movement) is the driving force that allows you to make a profit in any market. And the more you embrace the fact that real estate markets move in cycles — the more you let this repeating market occurrence sink deeply into your bones — the more you will be attuned to something that will allow you to make spectacular returns in real estate with little risk.

As good as this sounds, there *is* a slight catch.

Making money in real estate is never easy. The reason being lies in the fact that making a profit during times of change — especially a maximum profit from buying and selling at market turning points — requires you to be informed and prepared. But not everybody can be a big winner in real estate. For every informed seller who sells at an incredibly high price — on the other side of the deal — there is a corresponding, less informed buyer who overpays.

Sadly, while 99% of the general public does not know how to anticipate major trend changes in real estate markets, *The Campbell Method* for timing the real estate market will put you in the elite group of 1% who do. You should never forget that change is a double-edged sword: it creates both dangers, with risk of loss, as well as fantastic opportunities for profit. To build and protect wealth, you must be alert to each.

A Tale of Two San Diego Families

The 1990's were the best of times — and the worst of times — for San Diego homeowners. Here is a story of two similar families and the changing fortunes of the American dream.

In 1990, the San Diego real estate market was booming. Early in that year, Bob and Mary Armstrong purchased their suburban coastal home for $279,000. Times were good: the economy was strong and real estate prices were rising. But the good times soon turned bad. Over the next five years, property values fell sharply and the San Diego economy went into recession. Bob Armstrong eventually lost his job, which led to financial difficulties that forced him to sell the home in 1995. The market value had dropped to $184,000, a decline of 34%. Taking this price depreciation into account, the Armstrongs not only *lost* their original down payment of $55,800, but also *owed* the IRS $9,000 because the home sold for less than the amount of the mortgage (more about this later in this chapter).

It was John and Sally Robinson who bought the home from the Armstrongs in 1995 for $184,000. At that time there was a dark, black cloud hanging over the San Diego real estate market. Obscured by widespread pessimism, most people believed that prices would fall further. But it didn't turn out that way; the year 1995 turned out to be a *Stage One* market cycle bottom for San Diego real estate prices. During the next six years, there was a dramatic upsurge in property values. Because of a job transfer, the Robinsons had to sell their home in 2000. The value had climbed to $315,000, which was 71% higher than was originally paid. The Robinson's made a profit of $131,000, and as if that wasn't a reason for celebration by itself, this huge profit turned out to be 100% *tax-free* under the new tax laws! (Unlike the old tax laws, the new tax laws did not require the $131,000 profit to be re-invested in another home within 2 years to avoid paying taxes on the capital-gain profits.)

Reversal of Fortunes: What Changed?

As you read this story, you see that home ownership brought two families completely different results. What happened needs little in the way of explanation.

Did the length of home ownership change? No, it was five years for both families.

Did the location change? No, it was the same home.

But what *did* change was the trend of the market. After rising by 20% in 1988 and by 25% in 1989, San Diego real estate prices peaked in early 1990. Prices had risen too high, too fast, and were now headed for a dramatic fall. In other words, the *Stage Two* uptrend had ended and the *Stage Four* downtrend had started. While the "warning signs" were clearly there for informed market watchers to see, most people were caught by complete surprise. Prices eventually crashed by 25-40% before the San Diego real estate market hit bottom in 1995.

Unfortunately, Bob and Mary Armstrong bought in 1990 and sold in 1995. They bought at the *wrong time* and sold at the *wrong time*. They suffered a loss of $64,800 ($55,800 + $9,000).

But as day follows night, good markets follow bad markets.

After sinking lower and lower for five straight years, San Diego home prices had finally reached the point in the market cycle where they were a bargain. Foreclosures were rampant, and each month droves of people were walking into banks, turning in their keys, and walking away from properties that had more debt than value. Because of this, real estate auctions had become big business, and with hundreds of homes sitting vacant or abandoned, many were sold for as much as 50% below their already depressed market value. With the "blood running in the streets," this was clearly the time to buy.

With little fanfare, and amid fear and uncertainty, the real estate market was giving alert market-watchers clear "signals" that a trend reversal was near. In 1995, prices slowly and quietly started to rise. The downtrend was over, and a new market uptrend was in its beginning stages. As it turned out, property values rose by 55-75% between the years of 1995 and 2000, and the uptrend in San Diego real estate prices was still going strong into the year 2001.

Good fortune came to John and Sally Robinson because they bought their home in 1995 and then sold in 2000. Whether it was skill, intuition, or blind luck is anyone's guess. The more important point is that the Robinsons made a lot of money because of *good timing*. They bought at the *right time* when property values were at their lowest point in the cycle and ready to move higher. Hence, they made a $131,000 profit when they sold six years later.

Timing is Everything

While timing is important in most matters in life, timing is *critically* important in the quest for big real estate profits. Real estate is a good investment some of the time, and maybe even most of the time, but definitely not all of the time. Because property values tend to move higher in a "two steps forward, one step back" manner, you can make spectacular profits in real estate during rising markets, *but* you can also experience some equally spectacular losses during falling markets.

To avoid the dangers caused by these "one step back" price reversals, the principle of *timing* must be understood and acted upon. It isn't easy getting rich and it isn't easy keeping it. Making money in real estate is only one-half of the success formula; protecting your money from loss is the other half.

By now you might be thinking . . . what about the "location, location, location" principle that builders, realtors and the media like to repeat like a mantra . . . as the key to real estate riches? Is this the most critical factor? Even though it has become every-one's pet answer for success, this mantra is a *myth*. Sure, within any given city, it is true that location is important and some locations are better than others, but *rarely* is location the most important factor if you want to lower risk and maximize gains.

After all, Bob and Mary Armstrong's home in San Diego, California was in an excellent location. The home was in a newer, rapidly growing suburban area that was only a few miles inland from the white sandy beaches of the Pacific Ocean. But as history so often proves, even "location, location, location" is no defense against financial loss when you buy and sell at the wrong time.

Optimal Timing = Optimal Profits

Of course, your timing doesn't have to be "off" as much as it was for the Armstrongs to cost you money in real estate. For instance, let's say that you buy your home *too early* . . . while the real estate market is still in a decline. Or maybe you buy your home *too late* . . . after prices have already gone up for a year or two from the market bottom. Again, has the location changed? Of course not. *But it is still going to cost you.* Why? Because you could have bought the same home for less money by purchasing at or near the market bottom. Therefore, any amount you overpay is *lost profit* that could be in your bank account when you sell.

Poor market timing also costs you money on the sell side. If you sell too early, before real estate prices have peaked, or if you sell too late, after prices have fallen, you are limiting your potential profits. In short, any selling price that is less than the highest price you could receive at the market peak also results in lost profits.

Clearly, *timing* is the answer for creating and protecting wealth in real estate. People who know how to accurately identify changing "market trends" early, and are not late to take action and buy or sell at the lowest or highest prices, are the individuals who make–and will always make–the greatest returns in real estate.

But also remember that, like the weather, real estate markets must be looked at locally, not nationally. For the same reasons that it can be sunny in Chicago and raining in Miami, real estate prices can be trending lower in New York City and be trending higher in Los Angeles. While national trends do influence local trends, the "timing" for each local real estate market must be based on its own supply and demand factors.

With Low Inflation, Real Estate Timing is Key

"If a stock isn't going up, don't buy it," advised Will Rogers.

While overly simplistic, this same advice also applies to real estate: only buy when the trend is up. The problem with trends, however, is that they don't go up forever. Since 1980, and while the time periods vary by regional area, real estate trends have gone up for about three to five years and then stopped. The trend then reverses and prices go down for about three to five years.

To give you some historical perspective, prior to 1980, making money in real estate was relatively easy. All you had to do was buy a piece of property in a good location, hold on to it for a few years, and then sell for a big profit. Market knowledge or skill wasn't critically important. Even if you overpaid because you were a real estate novice or naïve, *inflation* soon bailed you out of your mistake and made lemonade out of lemons.

After 1980, however, the rules changed because inflation changed. Rising to 13-14% in 1980, the threat of "runaway inflation" forced the Federal Reserve Board to slam on the brakes and slow down the economy. To control inflation, the "Fed" raised interest rates to extreme levels. The prime-lending rate (which is the best short-term interest rate offered to a business from a bank) shot up to an astronomical 22%. The effect on the economy was immediate and devastating. The U.S. economy went into two recessions between 1980 and 1983. During that time, traditional inflation hedges like oil, gold, silver, *and real estate* all plummeted in value. Oil prices fell from $35 per barrel to below $10. Gold prices dropped from $850 per ounce to $450 in a matter of months. Silver prices did the same, falling from almost $50 per ounce to $15.

What happened to real estate prices? They got clobbered too. With the economy in recession and mortgage rates soaring from 9% to 17%, home-buyer demand dried up. Even though there was a scarcity of buyers, huge numbers of homeowners were forced to sell because of the hard economic times. The outcome was devastating to property values. The supply-demand imbalance caused housing prices to tumble all across the United States, and especially hard hit were California, Colorado, Texas, Florida, and the Northeast. As demand fell, home prices fell. Wealth that took decades to build was destroyed in a year or two. It wasn't until 1983-1985 that, area-by-area, real estate values finally hit bottom and prices started climbing higher again. But like in the aftermath of a strong hurricane, the damage was done.

In the 1980's and 1990's, because of persistent actions by the Federal Reserve Board to continue to fight inflation, the game changed. As they say in business, the cheese got moved. While timing is always important under any market conditions, with little or no inflation, it became necessary to play the real estate game by a new set of rules.

In non-inflationary markets that have continued past the year 2000, the principle of market timing — and not "location, location,

location"–becomes much more critical if you want to make money in real estate and avoid serious mistakes. Now more than ever, you need to be informed and watch market trends. And the direction the trend is moving will tell you whether your money should be invested in real estate . . . or whether your money should be in the bank — safely in cash — while you wait for the next low risk buying opportunity to ride the next uptrend to a new market peak.

Home Sweet Home . . . or Nightmare on Elm Street?

Even though a home is always a home, it is not always a good investment. While the long-term trend in real estate prices has been ever upward, this trend is interrupted every decade or so by periodic, and often severe, market setbacks.

While everybody seems to have his or her favorite rags-to-riches real estate story, it seems like very few like to think about — let alone talk about — the downside. This is because Americans tend to be eternal optimists. They are born with the belief that real estate will forever go up in value. At worst, they believe real estate prices just level off for a while before they start moving higher again.

The truth is, real estate may look like an easy game, but history proves otherwise. While more money has indeed been made in real estate than any other industry, it is also true that more money has been lost. The reason for this is that real estate is a leveraged investment, that is, it is purchased mostly with borrowed money. As trends rise and fall, the effect of leverage will magnify the bottom line results . . . either for you or against you.

For example, when you combine leverage with *rising* real estate values, you are tapped into a fantastic money making machine. This was the case with John and Sally Robinson when they purchased their San Diego home in 1995. With 71% appreciation, the Robinson's 20% down payment ($36,800) on their $184,000 home turned into a $131,000 profit. This was a total return of

356% on their investment over a six-year period. However, if the Robinsons had only put 10% down ($18,400), the effect of leverage would have doubled their return to 712%.

There is, however, no free lunch. Leverage cuts both ways. Those who live by the sword can also die by it, as this author personally learned in the early 1990's. When you are on the wrong side of real estate trends, when you combine leverage with *falling* real estate prices, "Home Sweet Home" can rapidly turn into "Nightmare on Elm Street."

This is what happened to Bob and Mary Armstrong. After they bought their San Diego home in 1990 for $279,000 with an 80% mortgage loan, the home went down in value by 34%. Not only did they lose all of their $55,800 down payment, but since the mortgage was greater than the sale price of the home, this "short sale" resulted in what is known as "debt relief." Under IRS tax laws, debt relief is taxable as ordinary income. Therefore, in addition to losing their $55,800 down payment, the Armstrongs also owed $9000 of income tax on money that was never received. This loss was *not* tax-deductible under IRS tax laws, making a bad situation even worse.

Shattering the "Location, Location, Location" Myth

It should now be clear that "location, location, location" is not the most important or only determining factor necessary to achieve the greatest success in real estate. Instead, a focus on "market trends" and "timing" are what is needed.

The importance of timing brings to mind the story of a horse owner who was talking to his veterinarian. "I don't understand it," the man complained. "Sometimes my horse runs fine and sometimes he limps badly. Can you help me?" Without hesitation, the vet replied, "When your horse runs fine, sell him."

"Running fine" applies to real estate as well as horses. A trend is only a trend for a period of time. *Sooner or later, the trend will change.* To lower risk and maximize returns, you must be able to read these *trend changes*. You must be skillful and flexible enough to invest with the trend while it is going up, and then sell when you have evidence the trend is going to end.

Is it possible, however, to foresee these trend changes *in advance*? Is it possible to take advantage of only the rising markets and somehow avoid the dangers of the falling markets?

The answer is a resounding "yes." You *can* develop an "advance warning system" that will alert you to — and thus prepare you for — future trend changes in real estate markets. When you use *The Campbell Method* for timing the market, these trend changes need not catch you off guard. Instead, they can be used to your greatest advantage.

In the next chapter, you are going to learn a time-tested method for telling when major trend changes are likely to happen. It has been called the "Billionaire's Secret." With this secret, you will learn how to make much more than a profit in real estate . . . you will learn how to make a *maximum profit* in real estate.

– Chapter 3 –

The Great Real Estate Discovery

The secret of success is knowing something that no one else does.
— Aristotle Onasis

On June 25, 1876, the scouts of General George Armstrong Custer returned with some information that a large number of Indians were massing at Little Big Horn. Because of his past success as a war hero and Indian fighter — and without taking time to analyze the facts further — an overconfident Custer quickly set out with his 250 soldiers to "surround" nearly 4,000 Indians.

This was a serious mistake.

What is the lesson to be learned here? Analyze the facts before making key decisions.

Like General Custer, buyers and sellers of homes are often guilty of equally foolish errors in judgment. For most, a home is their greatest financial asset. And even though a home is more than a pure investment, people do buy homes with the expectation of making a profit. Despite these expectations, most people *fail* to analyze critical market facts before making buying and selling decisions.

This, too, is a serious mistake.

The Rise and Fall of California Real Estate Prices

In California, real estate fluctuates as much as the stock market — both up and down. Since the 1970's, every ten years we have witnessed property values soar to incredible heights only to crash down afterward. Granted, each market correction was eventually exceeded by higher prices during the ensuing market upturn, but that doesn't mean that there weren't significant risks along the way. Real estate is a lot like car racing: to win the race, you have to finish the race.

Real estate can fall from grace just like anything else. In the early 1980's and early 1990's, there were huge numbers of California homeowners who lost most, if not all, of their money due to crashing real estate markets. To advise people of the potential risks — and to discourage lawsuits that try to shift the blame when trouble arrives — grant deeds in California should come with a warning label: *Market downturns may prove hazardous to human wealth.*

The risks notwithstanding, real estate has still been the *best* long-term investment for the average American family; there is no question about it. Looking back at the general upward course of price trends, there is reason to believe we will continue to see higher real estate prices in the future. However, prices seem to fall off of a cliff after every real estate boom. Timing, therefore, is *always* critical . . . regardless of the long-term trend.

To maximize all the upside real estate has to offer — and minimize the downside risk — you are now going to learn how I made an important market-timing discovery in 1993.

Good Houses, Bad Timing

With a successful background as a real estate broker, investor, and homebuilder since 1972, I was building an eight-home subdivision in San Diego. The year was 1989 and the real estate market was going like gangbusters. Home prices climbed by 20% in 1988 and were doing even better in 1989. Speculation was rampant. Prospective buyers for new homes often *camped out* for days — and sometimes weeks — in front of builder sales offices for the "opportunity" to buy a home. Some people camped out so they could sell their positions in line for $5,000 to $10,000 to even more eager homebuyers.

This new home development looked like it was going to be my most profitable real estate investment *ever.* By all appearances, I was in the right place at the right time with the right product to sell. If everything went perfectly, I was going to make a killing.

But things did not go perfectly. Times *were* good . . . but times change.

Instead of a big winner, my eight-home real estate development turned into a big loser. The market was booming, but as history shows us over and over again, a pin lies in wait for every market bubble. San Diego real estate prices peaked out in 1989 and started a rapid downhill slide. The "Boom of the 1980's" turned into the "Bust of the 1990's."

A relentless five to six year downtrend in property values brought on deflated hopes, failed dreams and new realities for almost everyone who owned real estate in California. Instead of making a killing, I got killed. The "bigger fool" theory was over. How bad was it? Let's put it this way: if it were a fight, somebody would have stopped it.

And I found little consolation in the fact that self-help books told me it is your failures — not your successes — that make you strong. While I am sure there is some truth to this, given the choice, I would rather skip this method of education. Frankly, I believe it is smarter and less expensive to learn from other people's mistakes and failures. It is devastating to lose a lot of money. And for 44 year-old Robert Campbell — with a wife, two children, a dog and a home with a big mortgage — this was no ordinary failure. It was an extraordinary one.

The 1990's California Real Estate Crash

Prior to starting construction in early 1990, the possibility of failure never crossed my mind. The eight homes I was building were appraised for $2.2 million in 1989. However, by the time all the homes were built and sold in 1991, the total sales price of all eight homes had dropped to $1.8 million. In other words, the average value of each home had dropped from $275,000 to $225,000 in less than two years!

This market downturn caught practically everyone by surprise — including the so-called "experts." It was the worst real estate crash since the Great Depression. Home prices plunged by 25-40% during the next five years. Land prices fell as much as 60%! Many real estate owners lost everything. Even those that survived the "crash" — and avoided going broke — *still* suffered huge financial losses.

Personally, I *lost* $204,000 of hard-earned capital. I also lost over three years of time during which I earned absolutely no income from all my hard work and had to live off of my savings. The loss caused from building these eight homes, coupled with the huge loss I suffered from my two vacant land partnerships mentioned earlier, caused a negative and far-reaching ripple effect. It created a major financial setback that would take me years and years to overcome.

However, after witnessing and surviving this real estate collapse, I did learn a valuable lesson. I learned that working hard was not enough to be successful in life . . . or in real estate. It is more important to work smart.

I Made a Promise to Myself: No More Big Mistakes in Real Estate

I vowed this kind of real estate disaster would not happen to me again. Unlike General Custer at the Little Big Horn, I promised myself that I would never be lulled into a false sense of security about real estate uptrends. Never again would I be *so sure* about rising property values that I would become mentally lazy and forget how the market can crash and burn like any other market. As the ancient Greeks so wisely observed, I was living proof that

> "Whom the gods would destroy they would first make over-confident."

Furthermore, I promised to never again rely on the real estate "experts." Based on population and job growth in California, the experts had all predicted continued "good times" in San Diego real estate right up to the time the bottom fell out of the market in 1990.

To add insult to injury, guess what the experts said *after* the market crash? "You should have sold last year." Great advice, huh? This kind of astute financial insight reminds me of Wall Street analysts who — seemingly without fail — tell you to "sell" *only* after the market (or a stock) has already plummeted. In either case, advice like this is like a doctor recommending medicine after the patient has died.

What it all comes down to is this: with 20/20 hindsight we are all experts. Then, it is easy to be smart. But 20/20 hindsight does-n't help you in the real world. To manage risk and protect profits, you have to look forward and make decisions. You have to anticipate real estate trend changes — and sell — *before* the boom turns into a bust.

The Challenge: To Predict Major Turning Points in the Real Estate Market

So my challenge became this: "Would it be possible to predict these major trend changes in the real estate market . . . before they became obvious to all?"

Frankly . . . I didn't know, but it got me thinking.

While attending college, I had developed an insatiable interest for learning how to make money in the stock market. I was fascinated by the strategies used by professional traders for knowing *when* to buy and sell for large and consistent profits.

After years of study, I had learned many of the "secrets" of these market wizards.

One secret, however, stood head and shoulders above the others: the most successful traders would watch certain *key* market indicators that would tell them — in advance — what direction the stock market was likely to go.

Armed with this market direction information, these skilled Wall Street traders were *then* able to position their capital for profit while at the same time avoiding most of the risk.

What an incredible advantage for making money in the stock market! And while many of these "forward-looking" indicators were not always perfect — their batting average was sufficiently high to make these savvy traders very, very wealthy.

I wanted to see if the same formula used in the stock market could be applied to trends in the real estate market. If it was possible, I could profit from the market up-trends . . . and then sell to avoid the market downtrends.

Looking for Market Clues

Like Sherlock Holmes investigating real estate cycles, the first thing I did was make a list of all the economic indicators that could possibly reveal clues as to the future direction of the local San Diego market. Notice I said *local*, not national. There is a big difference. Property values can be rising in one area of the United States and falling in another. In fact, it happens all the time, it is very common.

This is an important point, so let me explain it more fully.

In doing my research, it didn't matter to me what the coming real estate trends were in New York, Chicago, Salt Lake City, Phoenix or elsewhere. I wasn't going to invest there. I was *only* concerned about making money from the trends in San Diego real estate. Therefore, I knew I should *only* look at San Diego economic indicators if I wanted to zero in on the San Diego market.

It took me a few months to gather all of the San Diego economic data. I had hoards of data for almost everything under the sun. I accumulated historic data on San Diego home prices, unemployment rates, population trends, new home sales, existing home sales, home affordability indexes, new home building permits, vacancy rates, job growth, home foreclosures, inventory indexes, construction activity, income levels, time on the market statistics, mortgage defaults, and remodeling permits. There were probably a few more indicators I looked at but I think you get the idea. I had a lot of data to test. While some of the statistical data was sketchy and difficult to obtain, I wanted to be as scientifically thorough as possible in doing this research.

Of course, I also looked at interest rates. From my formal education in economics and business — as well as my previous stock market research — I knew that interest rates were one of the best, if not *the* best, economic indicators that any investor could watch. I knew interest rates would probably play an important role in predicting future market trends.

Then came the part that is a little complex.

As I said before, the first step was to collect this raw economic data for *each* economic indicator. Most of these statistics are reported on a month-to-month basis. The second step was to mathematically analyze the statistical data. Basically, I was looking for *trends* in the data that might possibly foretell future real estate trends. In some cases, I had 25 to 30 years of monthly economic data to analyze for each economic indicator!

Finally, as the last step in my analysis, I compared the historical *trends* of each of these economic indicators against the historical price *trends* for San Diego real estate. I was looking for *correlations* between (1) the trends in the economic data and (2) the trends in property values. Even more importantly, I was looking for trend correlations that would give *advance warning* of turning points in the real estate cycle.

Research Results were Conclusive: New Market Discovery

After weeks of testing and experimenting with the numbers, I made a very profitable discovery. Research results showed that a positive link exists between five key economic indicators — which I now call "Vital Signs" — and future price trends for the San Diego real estate market.

How accurate were the research results?

These five Vital Sign indicators correctly anticipated and "signaled" *every* major market peak — and *every* major market bottom — in the San Diego real estate market since 1982. As you will see in a moment, there were a total of seven trend change signals.

I felt like a wildcatter who had just struck oil. After this historical research, I had mathematical proof that the real estate market *does* indeed "tip its hand" and give off clear signals about impending trend changes in the marketplace. My conclusions were not based on economic theory or black magic. These Vital Sign indicators had proven their value by passing the supreme test of real-world experimentation. In other words, they work.

While all the Vital Sign indicators provide valuable clues for anticipating trends, some proved to be better "leading indicators" than others. Ranking them from strongest to weakest, here is the general order in which the Vital Sign indicators will usually (but not always) "lead" the market trends:

1. Existing home sales
2. New home building permits
3. Mortgage loan defaults
4. Foreclosure sales
5. Interest rates

Because some Vital Sign indicators are better trend "predictors" than others, these indicators are not likely to give "buying signals" or "selling signals" in the same month. Instead, like dominos, they tend to fall one-by-one until the *weight of the evidence* of a looming trend change becomes overwhelming. How these Vital Sign indicators give "signals," and how to use the "domino effect" of these signals to make well-timed buying and selling decisions, will be fully illustrated in Chapters 6, 7 and 8.

After analyzing the order in which *each* Vital Sign indicator gave signals of a coming trend change, I had another idea. To simplify matters, I combined the trend "readings" of each individual Vital Sign indicator into one composite buy/sell index. Thus, with a proprietary formula, I created the "Real Estate Crash Index."

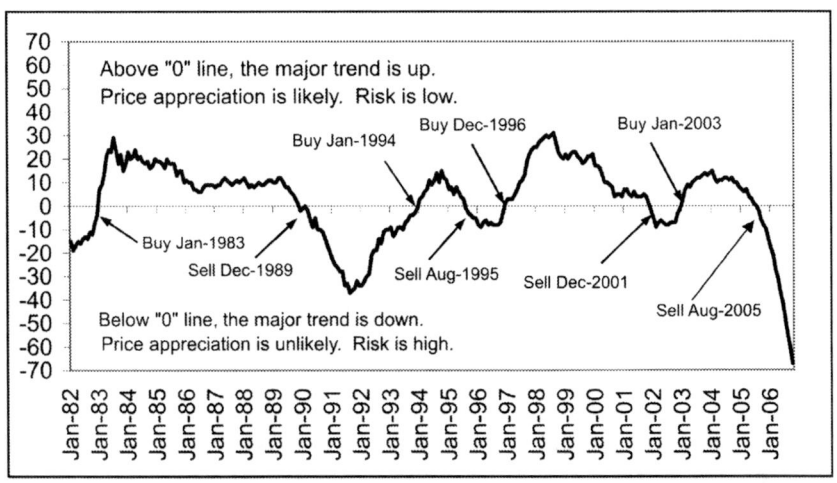

**Chart 3-1: The Real Estate Crash Index
San Diego County: 1982-2006**

Shown in Chart 3.1 above, this chart identifies those times when the combined readings of Vital Sign indicators flashed buy and sell signals for the San Diego real estate market.

Here is a log and evaluation of the seven signals given by the Real Estate Crash Index for the years 1982 to 2006.

Signal #1: After the real estate downturn in the early 1980's (caused by mortgage rates soaring to 17%), a buy signal came in January 1983. During the remainder of the 1980's, San Diego real estate prices rose by roughly 150-175% depending on the specific area.

Signal #2: After this huge rise in home prices in the 1980's, the Crash Index gave a sell signal in December 1989 for the San Diego real estate market. This signal to sell was about three to six months *before* the general public had any idea the previous market uptrend had reversed into a downtrend. Even *Barron's*, a highly respected financial publication that prides itself at "looking ahead" for the benefit of its readers, didn't catch wind of the trend change until it was obvious. In the July 23, 1990 issue, the *Barron's* headline read:

"Paradise Lost: California House Prices Are Slumping."

In retrospect, by following the Vital Sign indicators, I could have seen the 1990's San Diego real estate downturn coming. I could have sold the vacant land for my eight-home project—together with plans, permits and approvals — to a homebuilder who was unaware that the San Diego real estate market was peaking.

Signal #3 and Signal #4: After safely — and correctly — advising to steer clear of the worst San Diego real estate downturn since the Great Depression, the Crash Index gave a buy signal in January 1994 and a sell signal in August 1995. San Diego home prices, however, did not rise or fall very much after either of these two signals. Call it breakeven.

Signal #5: In December 1996, the Crash Index gave a buy signal for the San Diego real estate market. By the middle of the next year, home prices started to climb higher in a big way. By late 2001, San Diego home prices had risen by 80-100%.

Signal #6: In December 2001, the Crash index gave a sell signal for the San Diego real estate market. During the next 13 months, property values did not go down. Instead, home prices went up by about 20%.

This sixth signal illustrates why there is no Holy Grail for timing the market. That's why the goal is not perfection, but to increase profits and decrease risk by intelligently acting on likely probabilities as opposed to acting on whims and pure hope.

Signal #7: In January 2003, the Crash Index gave a buy signal for the San Diego real estate market. By the middle of 2005, which turned out to be the peak of this market upcycle, housing prices had risen by 80%.

Signal #8: In August 2005, the Crash Index gave a sell signal for the San Diego real estate market. As of the date of this Third Edition (January 2007), home prices had fallen 10–15% and are still declining.

NOTE: Market research shows that these buy and sell signals generated specifically for the San Diego housing market also apply to all Southern California housing markets. In fact, with only slight differences, history shows the timing signals for San Diego can even be applied to most major cities in all California. For the most current buy or sell signals for over 30 California cities, go to *www.CaliforniaRealEstateTiming.com.*

The Person with the Best Information Wins

Making money in real estate has always been a favorite American pastime. Whether you are a homeowner, a prospective homeowner or an investor, good market information is essential.

I wish I could rely on the news media, the economists and experts, or even real estate agents to give me the best information, but that is not the case. Most of these sources either are biased, are guessing, don't know where to look or, lastly, are guilty of assuming today's trend will continue forever.

History proves that trends only go so far before they change direction. From economic events, politics, actions of the Federal Reserve Board, new tax laws, and even changes in consumer behavior, the Vital Sign indicators take everything that can effect the market into account and tell you how the real estate market is reacting.

My research proved the market has the unique ability to send accurate and valuable information to buyers and sellers about what it is going to do next. Prices do not move from point A to point B by accident or chance, but do so for fundamental reasons that can be explained by *changes* in supply and demand. The market transmits these changes to you in its own special language, a language that is "decoded" by the Vital Sign indicators.

The Market is Blind to Individual Circumstances

The Campbell Method for tracking trends to buy and sell compels you to be market-centric, not egocentric. This is because the real estate market is completely impersonal and has no concern for individual circumstances. It is not for you or against you. It doesn't know if you own a home and want to sell it for the highest price, or if you want to buy a home for the lowest price.

If being impersonal isn't enough, the market goes one step further and takes full advantage of your weaknesses: greed, pride, fear, and ignorance. The market baits you into buying at the top of the cycle (greed), and scares you into selling at the bottom (fear). In other words, the market encourages you to do things that can prove to be costly and painful.

This means that your success in real estate will improve in direct proportion to the degree that you look at the market objectively and not emotionally. To accurately time the real estate market, *The Campbell Method* requires that you ignore what you hope and want the market to do . . . and focus instead on what the market is telling you to do.

Remember, whatever the prevailing trend is, you need to assume that that trend will continue until the market tells you otherwise. When the trend is going to change, the Vital Sign indicators will tell you — speaking to you in a language that is clear, easy to understand and honest.

Real estate trends matter, and your home will likely be the biggest investment you'll ever make. So why not use every advantage available to buy and sell at the most profitable times? While money isn't everything in life, there are some people who rank it right up there with oxygen. From personal experience, I believe Sophie Tucker may have said it best:

"I've been rich and I've been poor. Rich is better."

In the next chapter, each Vital Sign indicator will be described in detail. You are going to learn the simple logic behind their remarkable ability to foresee what is ahead for the real estate market. Buyers and sellers who follow these indicators will be greatly rewarded for their efforts.

– Chapter 4 –

The Five Vital Signs Indicators: Your Windows into the Future

Facts do not cease to exist because they are ignored.
— Aldous Huxley

Wouldn't it be great if there was a financial advisor you could count on?

If you want to make more money in real estate, the Vital Sign indicators are such an advisor. They tell you the truth about what is likely to happen next in the market. If you are a homeowner, they can tell you the most profitable time to sell. If you are a prospective homeowner, they can tell you the most profitable time to buy. If you are an investor, they can tell you how to make huge profits, as well as avoid losses.

The five Vital Sign indicators are the core of *The Campbell Method* for timing the real estate market. They are not based on fortune telling or knowing what the Federal Reserve Board is going to do to the economy. Instead, they work for the simple reason that markets are moved by people. And these key indicators focus *directly* on those people whose collective actions and behavior send real estate trends in motion.

Although it is popular to believe good markets and bad markets — booms and busts — occur "out of the blue" and "without warning," the Vital Sign indicators prove otherwise. Acting in the same way that a doctor gives a patient a medical check-up, these key indicators "take the temperature" and "read the pulse" of the market on a monthly basis, which clearly reveals clues as to whether the real estate market is likely to be healthy (or sick) in the future.

Eliminating the Cause and Effect Confusion

The trend will always move in the direction of the greatest market forces, which in turn create imbalances between supply and demand in the market. What is important to understand, however, is that you don't need to know the "causes" of these imbalances in order to figure out which way the trend is likely to go. Why? The reason is that the Vital Sign indicators are a *true reflection* of all market forces — both known and unknown — that are affecting the trend.

In short, the Vital Sign indicators simplify your ability to correctly analyze and anticipate future market trends. By giving you a month-to-month mathematical accounting of the battle between supply and demand, they tell you whether the buyers or the sellers are winning the war and hence which way property values are most likely to move.

Let's examine these forward-looking real estate indicators and see why they give you amazing insights into the future. Keep in mind that each Vital Sign indicator by itself only reveals a portion of the big picture. Combining them together reveals more.

Vital Sign Indicator #1: Existing Home Sales

Home sale activity is the best leading indicator of real estate price trends. This is because buyers create the demand for housing that is directly linked with price movement.

When the trend in existing home sales is increasing, more and more buyers coming into the marketplace. This increasing demand causes real estate prices to rise. Conversely, when the trend in existing home sales is decreasing, less and less buyers coming into the marketplace. This decreasing demand causes real estate prices to fall.

This is not to say that sellers aren't a factor in the supply and demand dynamics of real estate trends, but only that buyers play the more dominant role. The reason for this is that sellers can ask whatever price they want for homes, but until a buyer is willing to pay that price, they don't have a sale. This explains why home prices tend to go higher with increased buyer demand, and prices tend to fall with decreased buyer demand.

The laws of supply and demand are the determining forces behind the price of almost anything you can think of. It is one of the few examples of a practical, logical, and common sense principle to ever come from the study of economics. For this reason, if you only track one Vital Sign indicator, pay close attention to the trends in existing home sales. This is one of the true cornerstones for determining the direction of real estate prices. (See K.I.S.S. in Chapter 11.)

A key point to understand is that real estate prices don't go down because property owners decide to sell. Prices go down because people stop buying. That's why you should pay close attention to the volume of existing home sales, especially after a long market uptrend when real estate is high-priced and expectations are that prices will rise even higher.

Vital Sign Indicator #2: New Home Building Permits

To track real estate trends, new home building permits are important for two reasons. First, real estate construction is the largest single industry in the United States. It is estimated that 15-20% of the total US economy is tied to real estate construction. Thus, the fate of the economy — whether on a local or national basis — often hinges on the strength of the housing sector.

Secondly, new homebuilders are keenly aware of the demand for housing. When demand is strong, and new home sales are increasing, builders react by "pulling" more and more building permits to build new homes to satisfy the demand. When the demand is weak, and new home sales are decreasing, builders will pull fewer permits. They don't want to get stuck holding a lot of expensive housing inventory that is slow to sell. Builders know that new home sales are ruled by the same economic principle as existing home sales: *when demand falls, price reductions and loss of profits are likely to follow.*

There are 11 Leading Economic Indicators tracked by the U.S. Department of Commerce to measure the future strength or weakness of the U.S. economy. New Home Building Permits are one of the most accurate because historically, the trend in building permits starts to drop *before* the economy goes into recession, and the trend starts to rise *before* the economy starts to come out of recession.

To illustrate this relationship, look at Chart 4-1 on the next page. It compares New Home Building Permits and U.S. recessions, which are shown by shaded areas. This data confirms that New Home Building Permits are a leading indicator to the direction of the economy.

Vital Sign Indicator #3: Mortgage Loan Defaults

A mortgage is what you give the lender when you buy a home. It acts as the lender's security to make sure you will pay the debt. Basically, it is your pledge to make payments until the loan is paid off. If you pay the debt, everything is fine. If you don't pay the debt — meaning you have "defaulted" on your loan — there is a problem. To solve this problem, the lender can exercise its legal right to sell your home to satisfy the debt.

Mortgage loan defaults occur when a homeowner does not make a mortgage payment for a certain period of time — typically three to four months — and the lender records a "Notice of Default" against the property. This is the first step in the *foreclosure process*. It means that the property can be sold at a "foreclosure sale" if the borrower does not bring the mortgage current by paying the lender the delinquent mortgage payments.

The Five Vital Signs Indicators: Your Windows into the Future 57

Chart 4.1: U.S. Housing Starts

Trends in mortgage loan default are closely linked with real estate trends for two reasons.

First, the trend in loan defaults gives you a clear indication of the strength of the local economy. When mortgage loan defaults are decreasing, the economy is healthy, employment is strong, and most homeowners can likely make their mortgage payments with little difficulty. When mortgage loan defaults are increasing, this indicates the economy is weakening, unemployment is rising, and more and more people are having *serious* financial problems.

Secondly, the trend in mortgage loan defaults has direct implications for real estate prices. Homeowners who can't make their mortgage payments are generally under the gun to sell fast, usually at prices that are below current market value. If they don't sell fast, these defaulting homeowners risk losing much — if not all — of the equity in their home that will result from a bank foreclosure sale.

Simply stated, when loan defaults are increasing, real estate prices tend to decline. When loan defaults are decreasing, real estate prices are likely to rise.

Vital Sign Indicator #4: Foreclosure Sales

A foreclosure sale occurs when a mortgage lender is forced to sell a borrower's property in order to pay off the mortgage obligation that is in default. In states like California that use a Deed of Trust as security for the borrower's mortgage, a foreclosure sale is scheduled three months and 21 days (the minimum time period required by law) from the time the Notice of Default is recorded by the lender.

A rising trend in foreclosure sales has several implications for the local real estate market and the local economy . . . all of which are bad.

First, when foreclosures are rising, the demand for real estate is declining. Otherwise, to protect their home equity from being lost, the owners of properties in foreclosure would normally be able to sell *before* the bank was forced to auction off the property.

Secondly, when foreclosures are rising, real estate prices are likely to fall. This happens because people who buy at foreclosure sales are bargain hunters, typically buying at prices generally 15-20% below current market value. Thus, the greater the number of foreclosure sales, the greater the downward price pressure on the *entire* real estate market in any given area. After all, why buy retail when it is possible to buy wholesale?

Thirdly, when foreclosures are rising, it is a clear sign that the economy is weakening and that more and more people are having *severe* financial problems. Because the health of the real estate market is closely connected with the health of the economy, a slowing economy has a depressing effect on real estate prices.

On the other side of the coin, when trends in foreclosure sales are decreasing, this is a good sign for the economy and the real estate market. A declining number of foreclosure sales means the economy is strengthening and the demand for real estate is increasing. With fewer people and fewer properties in distress, home prices are more likely to rise.

Be aware that foreclosure sales are likely to be a lagging indicator at market peaks; however, they *may* be a coincidental indicator at market bottoms. Because market bottoms tend to take more time to develop than market peaks, Vital Sign indicator #4 is *far more likely* to help market-watchers buy low than to sell high.

Vital Sign Indicator #5: Interest Rates

Interest rates affect property values in a similar same way that gravity acts on physical objects. The higher rates climb, the greater the downward pressure on prices. In contrast, falling interest rates have an uplifting effect on real estate prices.

Here is an example of why lower mortgage rates tend to stimulate the housing market and increase home values. Assume interest rates fall from 9% to 7%. Based on your income, let's say you can qualify for a $150,000 mortgage at 9% interest rate. The payment on this loan (principle and interest only) would be $1207 per month.

With a 7% interest rate and the same income, however, you could now qualify for an $181,000 mortgage. Your payments would remain the same as before at $1207 per month. In other words, with a 2% drop in interest rates, the value of that same home could theoretically increase by $31,00) — or roughly 21% — without you having to increase your monthly payment.

Of course, the interest rate effect cuts both ways. When interest rates rise, borrowers can now qualify for smaller loans. This puts downward pressure on property values.

How Interest Rates Fit into The Campbell Method

Unlike Vital Sign indicators #1 through #4, which are all driven by market forces *specific* to a major metropolitan area, local market forces *do not* determine interest rates. Instead, interest rates are driven by national — or even global — economic conditions.

So how does Vital Sign indicator #5 fit into *The Campbell Method* for real estate timing?

While interest rate trends *do* have a predictable impact on home affordability and property values, as well as strength of the local economy, market research shows that they *do not* impact the major trend of the market as significantly as the other Vital Sign indicators. Hence, even though trends in interest rates are useful in gauging the *potential* strength — or weakness — that may be developing in the market, as a predictor of real estate trends, interest rate trends should not be judged alone. They need to be used in *conjunction* with the other Vital Sign indicators. For example:

- When Vital Sign indicators #1 through #4 are signaling an *upward trend* in real estate prices, rising interest rates tend to slow the uptrend down . . . and falling rates tend to speed up the rise in prices.

- When Vital Sign indicators #1 through #4 are signaling a *downward trend* for real estate prices, rising interest rates tend to speed up the downtrend . . . and falling rates will tend to slow down the decline.

It should be noted that during *Stage Two* market upcycles (page 19), falling interest rates frequently act like a shot of adrenaline into the market. This is the "sweet spot" in the real estate cycle. It is here where home values can appreciate rapidly and it is definitely a time when you want to own real estate.

In short, while there is always a dynamic and an on-going interaction between interest rates and the other Vital Sign indicators, only indicators #1 through #4 give specific buy and sell signals that you can act on with a high degree of confidence; interest rates do not. Therefore, to factor this into *The Campbell Method*, interest rate trends should be viewed as an accelerator — or brake — to what the other Vital Sign indicators are telling you about the general market trend.

The Vital Sign Indicators are the Market's Weathervane

In weather forecasting, scientists use barometers to measure changes in atmospheric pressure, which in turn acts as an "indicator of change" to future weather conditions.

Similarly, the Vital Sign indicators are *market barometers* for trend forecasting in real estate. They measure supply and demand changes that will lead to changes in market conditions. It is equally interesting to note that while the weatherman's barometer and the Vital Sign indicators do not tell you the *cause* of change, they do identify those specific conditions that *lead* to change.

You now have a simple and powerful set of indicators to forecast future real estate trends. In fact, you have to try very hard not to believe what these Vital Signs are telling you. And even though no market indicators are infallible, it is hard to imagine that any major real estate uptrend — or downtrend — could ever begin without these Vital Sign indicators flashing warning signals well in advance.

So why try to out-think or out-smart the real estate market when you don't have to? Instead, these Vital Sign indicators represent *pure factual data* about what is going on in the market. They see the market as it is — not as we hope or want it to be.

And if you only learn one thing from *The Campbell Method*, learn this: with real estate trends, you might not know "why" something is happening, but the Vital Sign indicators do tell you "what" is happening . . . and "what" is all that matters.

— Chapter 5 —

The World's First Billionaire Shares His Secret

*If you can keep your head when those all about you are losing theirs . . .
Yours is the Earth and everything that is in it.*
— Rudyard Kipling

Oil tycoon J. Paul Getty was one of the most successful businessmen the world has ever seen. Worth an estimated $3 billion when he died in 1976 at the age of 83, Getty divulged his simple formula for acquiring great wealth. In his autobiography, *How to Be Rich*, he wrote:

> If you want to make money, really big money, do what nobody else is doing. Buy when everyone else is selling and hold until everyone else is buying. This is not merely a catchy slogan. It is the very essence of successful investment.

What does this mean if you want to make "really big money" in real estate? Knowing that real estate is cyclical means that when prices are pushed too far in one direction because of overwhelming public opinion, you must do the opposite of what everybody else is doing. This is known as "contrary thinking." It's the ability to think and act objectively and independently, and not be influenced by the pressures of the crowd.

That sounds a little crazy, you say? Sell your property when everyone is buying? Then buy when everyone is selling? Contrary thinkers like Getty and other wealthy people know otherwise. They are not just trying to be different. Instead, they know that to get ahead in life, you must follow one simple rule: buy low and sell high. Applying this rule to real estate, common sense tells us that if everybody wants to buy, real estate is likely to be *expensive*. Conversely, if nobody wants to buy, real estate is likely to be *cheap*.

While the laws of supply and demand are the market forces that determine price trends, *mass crowd psychology* — fear and greed — is what drives prices to unreasonable extremes. Here is how these two powerful emotions operate at the tail end of market trends:

- An upward trend in prices turns into a stage of euphoria and greed, resulting in property becoming *overpriced*.

- A downward trend in prices turns into a stage of gloom and fear, resulting in property becoming *underpriced*.

As Getty explained, you don't get rich by following the crowd. If it were that simple, everyone would be rich. To beat the crowd, therefore, you have to look at the market differently than the crowd. This means that when the crowd — the general public — is ruled by impulsive behavior and emotions, the high profit real estate investor must be unemotional and calm, look at the market objectively, and act only after careful analysis.

The Herd Instinct

Why does contrary thinking work? It works because most people are followers, not leaders. In other words, people find great comfort in running with the herd. That explains why most people buy only after they see others buying. Then they wait to sell only after they see other people selling.

While taking advantage of trends is the key to making money in the markets, the problem is that the general public tends to act late . . . often dangerously late.

In fact, based on the "herd instinct" in human beings, most people will wait until there is almost "incontestable proof" that market conditions have changed before they buy or sell. When prices are going up, they wait until they see others making big money before they buy. Then, when prices are going down, they wait until they see others losing big money before they sell. Either way, chasing the crowd costs the average person a lot of money: he or she buys late and pays too much, and sells late for too little.

Human nature being what it is, during a real estate uptrend, the higher that prices rise, the more the crowd becomes consumed with greed and visions of "easy profits." They become far more concerned with missing out on big profits than protecting their money from loss. Typically, many act on a "sure thing" at exactly the wrong time, when risk is greatest.

In a real estate downturn, as prices fall lower and lower, varying degrees of fear eventually seize the crowd. Near the market bottom, when the crowd believes all hope is lost, many people wrongly throw in the towel and sell at a time when further risk of loss is virtually zero.

Without question, being "in" with the crowd gives people a sense of security. However, to fight this powerful temptation to follow the crowd, you must realize that facts don't change just because you're not looking at them. In other words:

Even though 20 million people may believe or do a foolish thing, it's still a foolish thing.

In the real estate market, acting foolishly means ignoring risk at market tops. It also means not recognizing opportunity at market bottoms. For example, at market bottoms, when doom and gloom are pervasive, real estate can often be bought for as low as 50% of its previous value. At market tops, when everyone is irrationally exuberant and the future looks bright, people often rush to buy your real estate for 50-150% more than you paid for it. If you sheepishly follow the crowd and do what everyone else is doing, you will lose out. Why? Because it is unlikely that you will take advantage of these great buying and selling opportunities.

Following the crowd is the easy thing to do but it is never the most profitable. Business writer Mark Johnson neatly sums up the reason for this:

"The market doesn't reward qualities that are not scarce."

Buying into market weakness and selling into market strength is never easy. It takes extraordinary will power and self-discipline . . . and courage. Yet even though the contrary thinker's adage of "selling when it's hot" and "buying when it's not" goes totally against human nature, this is what you must do to make the biggest real estate profits.

The Mood of the Market

If there is one thing that disco, professional football in Los Angeles, and Elizabeth Taylor's marriages have taught us, it is that nothing lasts forever. Knowing that all real estate trends eventually change direction, the key to profiting from contrary thinking is to understand market psychology. The first step in doing this is to understand that people are what make markets.

Because people make markets, it is logical to conclude that just as people go through mood swings, so do markets.

Richard Band, in his book *Contrary Investing*, describes this phenomenon of changing market moods: "When prices are rising, the market's mood turns increasingly optimistic. The opposite happens when prices are falling, the market's mood turns increasingly pessimistic."

As shown in Chart 3-1, when real estate is underpriced at *Stage One* market bottoms, prices slowly start to rise out of a climate of fear. As prices continue to move higher, fear disappears, and is replaced by an attitude of caution. Then, as the real estate uptrend picks up steam and prices move noticeably higher, the painful memory of the market's last downturn gradually fades away. Confidence now prevails in the marketplace. "Finally, as prices reach a cyclical peak," says Band, "euphoria sweeps the market. At the top, all but a handful of people are convinced that the market will keep going indefinitely."

The same sequence of emotions occur during real estate downtrends, except in reverse order. Prices start to fall from a climate of euphoria at *Stage Three* market peaks, when real estate is overpriced. Then, at the market cycle bottom, when almost everyone expects prices to collapse further, the market becomes governed by fear.

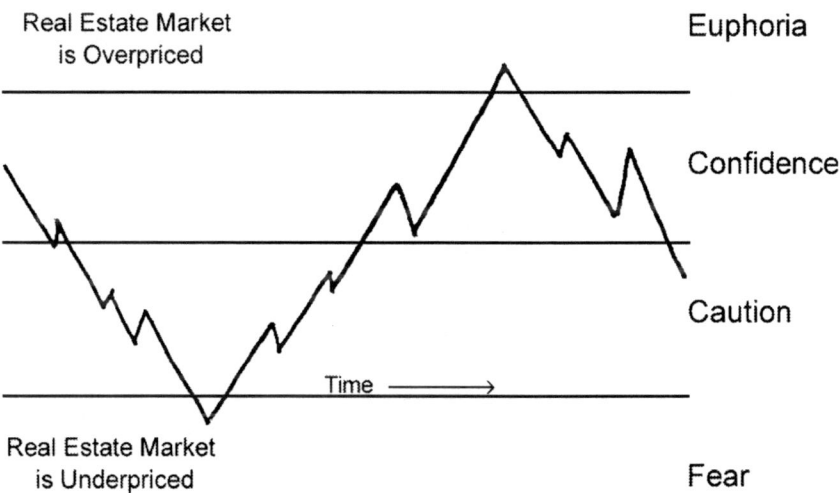

Chart 5-1: Mood of the Market

Where "Bad" News is "Good" News . . . and Visa Versa

To profit from these mood swings in the market, the contrary thinker must constantly fight off the temptation to become more pessimistic as prices fall. Actually, you should be happy as prices move lower. Why? Because as home prices fall, you know the market is getting closer to a bottom where you will have the opportunity to buy cheaply.

By the same token, you should guard against becoming overly optimistic as prices rise. Instead, as prices increase, contrary thinkers should become increasingly nervous. You know the higher prices rise, the closer the market is to reaching a peak. This, of course, is the time to sell.

Remember this: wealth is never permanent. Money has wings. What the market gives you today can be taken away from you tomorrow. As you learned in Chapter 2, a good location is not always synonymous with profits. Good timing is.

Is the Crowd Always Wrong?

The contrary approach is largely a matter of thinking clearly for yourself. It encourages you to use your brain and see what the crowd can't see, or is too slow to see. And contrary thinking isn't just some crazy, negative philosophy. As Johann von Goethe, the great German poet-philosopher, once wrote:

"I find more and more that it is well to be on the side of the minority, since it is always the more intelligent."

But is the crowd always wrong? To buy and sell at the most profitable times, should you always zig when the crowd zags? Is this the simple Getty formula?

No, unfortunately, it is not quite that easy. Even though the crowd is wrong some of the time, it is not wrong all of the time. As Gustave Le Bon explains in *The Crowd*, his 1895 classic on mass psychology, "A crowd goes from controlled logic to uncontrolled emotion." Translated into market behavior, this means you can count on the crowd to be right during the middle of trends, *but wrong at the end of trends.*

This important point bears repeating: the crowd is right during the trends — but wrong at the ends. And if you think about it for a second, this makes perfect sense. During the "middle" part of real estate trends, almost anybody can calmly and objectively look around and tell what direction prices are moving. But at the end of trends, when the market is bubbling with optimism or gripped by pessimism, the powers of fear and greed can easily overrule rational and intelligent decision-making.

Therefore, the time that it counts most to be right — meaning selling at market cycle peaks and buying at market cycle bottoms — this is the time that you can count on the crowd to be consistently wrong.

How to Gauge the Market's Psychological Mood

With so much riding on the correct decision as when to buy and sell, each person must define at what point in time to "go contrary" to public opinion. Like a pendulum that swings from excessive optimism to excessive pessimism, the trick is to determine when the crowd's most extreme level of emotion is reached.

The easiest way to gauge public opinion and the mood of a real estate market is to read *local* newspapers and magazines. These are good indicators because the press is in the business of selling stories. They basically report what the general public wants to hear. At market peaks, the press tells the public that everything is great and it will get better in the future. At the bottom, the press reports that not only have they never seen things this bad, but that they will only get worse.

In fact, the press and the general public actually feed off of each other at market cycle extremes. Once the public reads about a popular trend in the press, they become even more convinced the trend will continue. This fuels even greater conviction about the market's direction . . . and the trend gets even stronger.

It really is amazing. At market peaks, the press believes that if three buyers are eager to overbid each other to the point where the winner gets to pay $15,000 over market value, this is a sign of a good, healthy real estate market. Then, at market bottoms, when the bank is selling the same property for 30-40% less than it was purchased for five years earlier, the press writes about how terrible the market is.

At this point, you are likely nodding your head in approval of J. Paul Getty's contrarian investment formula. It makes a lot of sense, right? Yet to put this formula into practice, you still have to overcome a key market-timing question: how can you determine *the* most profitable time to go contrary to the crowd?

The Campbell Method: Turning the Art of Contrary Thinking Into a Science

The problem with contrary thinking has always been that high levels of optimism and pessimism can sometimes last for *years* before trend reversals actually occur. This phenomenon makes contrary thinking an art as much as a science for market timing purposes — forcing you to make subjective decisions for determining the most profitable times to buy and sell.

With no objective way to signal imminent trend reversals, from a practical standpoint, the main purpose of the "contrary approach" has always been to have you thinking — and leaning — in the *opposite direction* as the general public becomes more and more *unanimous* in their outlook for the market.

So how do you identify the best possible time to break away from the crowd and go in the other direction?

With *The Campbell Method* for tracking trends to buy and sell, you can now use the Vital Sign indicators to more scientifically identify the best time to "go contrary to the crowd." These key mar-ket-timing indicators objectively measure when trends are likely to change and, as a result, allow you to more accurately apply J. Paul Getty's great wealth formula to real estate cycles.

– Chapter 6 –

Calculating Vital Sign Trends: Don't Sweat the Math

The facts, Ma'am. Just the facts.
— Sergeant Joe Friday (Dragnet)

According to the rules of timing, there is no such thing as a bad piece of real estate. There are only good pieces of real estate that are owned at a bad time.

So how do we identify future real estate trends?

While it is impossible to know what tomorrow's newspaper will say, you do know what happened yesterday. And when you compare market data for what happened yesterday against market data for what happened today, you can measure change that has already taken place in the market. If you correctly interpret this information, the market will give you valuable trend information that you can profit from.

To identify changing real estate trends, the market data you will be keying on is the *Vital Sign data*. Comparing current Vital Sign data against that from the recent past tells you "the trend" for each of these indicators. And once you know which way these Vital Sign trends are going, you will know which way the major trend of the market is likely to go.

This chapter gives you two simple formulas that can keep you ahead of market trends. Don't worry if you don't know how to chart a market indicator or read a graph. Using some basic math that you learned in grade school, you can follow step-by-step instructions on how to calculate Vital Sign trends.

Predicting the Future?

Before you learn how to calculate Vital Sign trends, it is important to keep in perspective what these indicators can and cannot do. On the surface, it might appear that these indicators are capable of predicting the future. This isn't the case. In actuality, these indicators are merely predicting trend changes that are already in motion. So what is the advantage? The advantage comes from your ability to detect trend changes *early* — usually three to six months *before* the general public becomes aware of them.

Even though the "forward vision" of these indictors is nearsighted at best, this is not a serious limitation. Why? Because real estate markets tend to rise and fall in long, steady, well-defined trends. Like an oil tanker under full power at sea, the general trend of property values is likely to continue moving in a direction that is not easily reversed. Therefore, even though real estate trends carry no guarantees of time, once the Vital Sign indicators signal a change of trend, odds are strong that this new trend will last for years and years.

The bottom line is that the Vital Sign indicators *cannot* predict the distant future. Instead, visualize them like headlights on a car: they can help you to see down the road, but not around the corner.

Identifying Trends and Trend Changes:
The Principle of Market Momentum

In 1686, Sir Issac Newton discovered that "an object in motion tends to stay in motion until it encounters an opposing force." If you throw a ball up into the air, for example, it will continue to go higher and higher until the opposing force (gravity) causes the ball to fall back to earth.

By scientifically measuring momentum in the real estate market, Newton's law of motion can also be applied to tracking real estate trends. For this reason, once real estate prices start to trend (i.e. move) either up or down, they are likely to continue to trend in that same direction until opposing market forces — namely, changes between the forces of supply and demand — intervene and cause the trend to move in the opposite direction.

Thus, with monthly data from each of the five Vital Sign indicators, *The Campbell Method* uses "market momentum" as its primary statistical tool for tracking real estate trends.

Charting the Market's Momentum

What momentum actually measures is the "speed" at which an object is moving in a given direction. To illustrate this, visualize the motion of a swinging pendulum. As the pendulum swings back and forth — just like real estate cycles swing — it is easy to see (and understand) that before the pendulum can change direction, the speed at which it is traveling must first slow down and then come to a complete stop.

Like all moving objects, markets also have momentum.

This means that just as you can anticipate when a pendulum is going to change direction by measuring its speed of movement (i.e. slowing down before it comes to a complete stop), you can also anticipate when the trend of the real estate market is going to change direction by measuring the speed of movement of the Vital Sign indicators.

While real estate trends are not as precise as the back and forth movement of a pendulum, the same principles of momentum apply. To illustrate how *The Campbell Method* uses market momentum for real estate timing purposes, refer to Chart 6-1 on the next page.

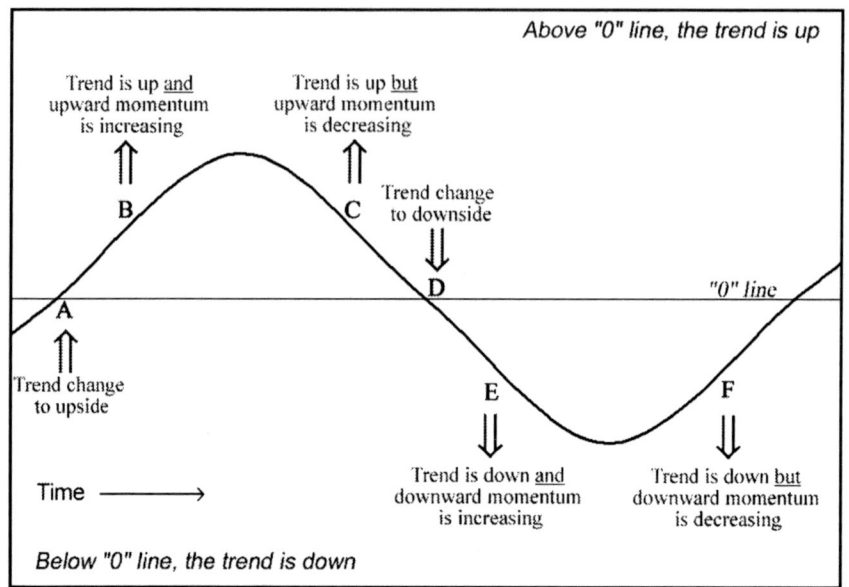

Chart 6-1: Market Momentum (Idealized)

How do you interpret a market momentum chart?

First, when the market momentum "trend reading" is *above* the "0" line — this means the Vital Sign indicator being charted is in an uptrend. When the trend reading is *below* the "0" line, the Vital Sign indicator is in a downtrend.

Secondly, trend changes are signaled when the "0" line is crossed in either direction. If the trend reading has been below the "0" line and then crosses above the "0" line, this means the trend of this Vital Sign indicator has changed from a downtrend to an uptrend. On the other hand, a drop from above to below the "0" line means just the opposite.

Thirdly, regardless of whether the trend reading for a Vital Sign indicator is above or below the "0" line, the direction the trend reading is moving tells you if the prevailing trend is gaining momentum or losing momentum. Thus, as the "0" line is approached, this type of market observation can help you anticipate possible market reversals even earlier.

Now that you are familiar with how to interpret these market momentum charts, refer to Chart 6-2 below. This is a chart of Vital Sign indicator #4: foreclosure sales for San Diego County from 1984 to 2001. Take a moment to get familiar with it because Chart 6-2 is an example of the charts you will see in Chapter 7: The Best Time to Buy and Chapter 8: The Best Time to Sell.

Important note: Bear in mind that market timing signals for each Vital Sign indicator only give you *one piece* of the puzzle of predicting trend reversals. As you will learn in the next three chapters, some Vital Sign indicators are stronger than others for signaling trend changes, and also, it is far wiser to act on multiple trend change signals than to act on only one. (This is why the Real Estate Crash Index blends all five Vital Sign indicators into one buy/sell indicator.)

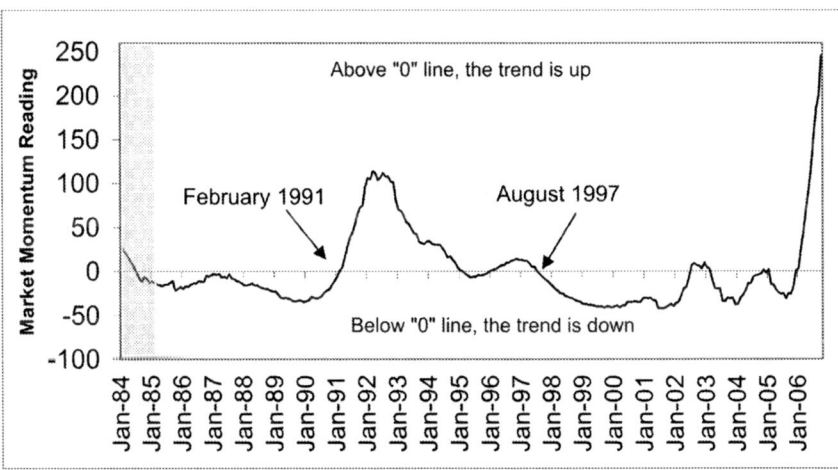

Chart 6-2: Market Momentum (Actual)
Foreclosure Sales for San Diego, CA, 1984-2006

(Note: This author offers software that automatically calculates and charts the market momentum trend readings for the Vital Sign indicators. To find out how to order the Market Momentum software, see page 191.)

Speaking the Same Language

Before you learn how to calculate market momentum, here are a few terms and definitions you must learn:

Trend: This refers to the general direction (up or down) in which a Vital Sign indicator is moving.

Moving Average (MA): This calculation gives you a "monthly average" for Vital Sign data over a selected period of time. A moving average is important because it "moves" the way the market moves — smoothing out the erratic month-to-month fluctuations — and thus it gives you a good general sense of the direction in which a trend is moving.

Market Momentum: This is the key statistical tool used to measure the trend of a Vital Sign indicator. It also measures whether the trend is speeding up (getting stronger) or slowing down (getting weaker). Market momentum is able to predict major market turning points (trend changes) in advance of the actual rise or fall of prices.

Uptrend: The condition that occurs when the market momentum calculation of a Vital Sign indicator is above the "0" line. Depending on the Vital Sign indicator, an uptrend is either a good sign — or a bad sign — for the market in general.

Downtrend: The condition that occurs when the market momentum calculation of a Vital Sign indicator is below the "0" line. Depending on the Vital Sign indicator, a downtrend is either a good sign — or a bad sign — for the market in general.

Trend Identification:
It's as Easy as One, Two, Three

Identifying the trend of each Vital Sign indicator is a three-step process. The first step is accumulating monthly market data. Steps two and three require the application of some simple math to convert this raw — and sometimes erratic — monthly data into meaningful trends that you can profit from. Always understand that *The Campbell Method* is specifically designed to identify the beginnings and endings of long-term real estate trends — and ignore short-term market fluctuations.

As shown on Chart 6-3 below, which is a worksheet that shows you how to calculate market momentum, here is a description of each of the three steps:

Step One: Keep a log of the monthly data for each Vital Sign indicator. (Columns A, B and C)

Step Two: After you have collected a minimum of 12 months of

data, calculate the 12-month moving average for each Vital Sign indicator. (Column D)

Step Three: After you have numerical entries for 12 months of moving averages, calculate the momentum reading for each Vital Sign indicator. (Column E)

Chart 6-3: Market Momentum Worksheet, San Diego Foreclosure Sales, 1982-1984

Column A Month	Column B Month and Year	Column C Vital Sign Monthly Data	Column D 12-month Moving Average	Column E Vital Sign Momentum Reading
1	Jan-1982	190		
2	Feb-1982	179		
3	Mar-1982	251		
4	Apr-1982	223		
5	May-1982	206		
6	Jun-1982	260		
7	Jul-1982	238		
8	Aug-1982	268		
9	Sept-1982	287		

Column A Month	Column B Month and Year	Column C Vital Sign Monthly Data	Column D 12-month Moving Average	Column E Vital Sign Momentum Reading
10	Oct-1982	366		
11	Nov-1982	309		
12	Dec-1982	306	257	
13	Jan-1983	283	265	
14	Feb-1983	302	275	
15	Mar-1983	339	282	
16	Apr-1983	338	292	
17	May-1983	343	303	
18	Jun-1983	357	311	
18	Jul-1983	357	321	
20	Aug-1983	423	334	
21	Sept-1983	334	338	
22	Oct-1983	321	334	
23	Nov-1983	306	334	
24	Dec-1983	368	339	32
25	Jan-1984	243	336	27
26	Feb-1984	301	335	22
27	Mar-1984	346	336	19
28	Apr-1984	304	333	14
29	May-1984	307	330	9
30	Jun-1984	257	322	4
31	Jul-1984	271	315	-2
32	Aug-1984	293	304	-9
33	Sept-1984	235	296	-12
34	Oct-1984	532	314	-6
35	Nov-1984	209	306	-9
36	Dec-1984	229	294	-13

Step One: Collect Monthly Vital Sign Data

For each Vital Sign indicator, keep a log to record the monthly data. See Columns A, B and C on Chart 6-3. Instructions on where to locate this Vital Sign data will be covered shortly.

Step Two: Calculate Moving Averages

The purpose of a moving average is to "smooth out" raw market data and make it easier to identify the underlying trend. A moving average (MA) is calculated as follows: add up the data for the period of time that you want to average and then divide this total by the time period that you have selected. For our specific purposes, we are going to calculate (and maint0ain) an on-going 12-month moving average for each Vital Sign indicator.

The formula for calculating a 12-month moving average (MA) is:

The sum of months 1 through 12 ÷ 12 months

To show how this is done, look at Chart 6-3 — which is a monthly log of Vital Sign data for foreclosure sales. To calculate a 12-month MA, add up the oldest 12 months of data (months 1 to 12) and divide the total by 12. In December 1982, for example, the 12-month moving average is 257. Going to Column D, month 12, you can see this where the calculation is recorded on the Market Momentum Worksheet.

To continue these moving average calculations for the following months, you simply repeat the same procedure with each new month of Vital Sign data. For example, to calculate the 12-month moving average for January 1983, you add months 2 through 13 and divide the total by 12. The 12-month moving average for January 1983 now becomes 265 (Column D, month 13). As you can see, the MA increased from 257 to 265 from one month to the next. This occurred because month 1 (190 foreclosures) was dropped from the moving average calculations . . . and month 13 (283 foreclosures) was added.

By design, as these calculations show, the moving average "moves" in step with the 12 most current months of Vital Sign data. This gives you your first important indication as to whether the real estate market is getting stronger or weaker.

Step Three: How to Calculate Market Momentum

Once you complete Step Two for 13 continuous months (see Chart 6-3, Column D, month 24), you can start to calculate the market momentum readings for the specific Vital Sign you are tracking. To do this, two steps are required. First, from Column D, you subtract the most current 12-month moving average from the 12-month moving average that was calculated in the same month, but one-year prior. Second, you divide this number by the 12-month moving average of the previous year.

The formula for calculating market momentum is:

**Current 12-month MA — Previous Year 12-month MA)
÷ Previous Year 12-month MA**

Referring to Chart 6-3 again, you subtract the moving average (MA) from one year ago (Column D, month 12) from the more current MA one year later (Column D, month 24). Using the actual numbers, you subtract 257 from 339. The difference is +82. You now divide +82 by 257, and this results in a market momentum reading of +32 for December 1983. This calculation is recorded in Column E, month 24.

For December 1983 (actual date not shown on chart), notice that +32 is the first market momentum reading that is plotted on Chart 6-2.

In the same way that moving averages are calculated, this procedure for calculating market momentum is repeated with each new month of Vital Sign data. For January 1984, for example, you subtract the MA from month 13 (265) from the MA of month 25 (336) and divide this number by the MA from month 13 (265).

Thus, 336 -265 = 71...and when you divide 71 by 265, this results in a market momentum reading of +27 for January 1984.

For January 1984, note that +27 is the next market momentum reading that is plotted on Chart 6-2.

To show you how this procedure is continued with each new month of Vital Sign data, the highlighted portion of Chart 6-2 shows the actual market momentum readings that are plotted from the calculations shown in Chart 6-3, Column E. As you can see, these market momentum readings are plotted above or below the "0" line. If the readings are above the "0" line, this means that the Vital Sign indicator is in an uptrend. If the readings are below the "0" line, this means that the Vital Sign indicator is in a downtrend.

Note: All market momentum calculations shown in this book have been multiplied by 100 to eliminate the decimal point.

Important Time Periods Used with The Campbell Method

There are good reasons why 12 months of Vital Sign data are used in the moving average calculations in Step Two, and year-to-year comparisons (between these moving average calculations) are used for the market momentum readings calculated in Step Three.

First, whichever Vital Sign indicator you are tracking, be aware that two or three months of market data *do not* make a trend. Even though the news media likes to sensationalize stories with headline grabbing statistics, when you only look at a month or two of data, it is prudent to be as skeptical about the good numbers as it is about the bad numbers. Just as it takes a mile or two to turn an oil tanker around, real estate markets tend to turn slowly as well.

Secondly, in tracking major trends, there is a seasonal aspect to real estate activity that needs be taken into account. There are more home sales in the summer months and less in the winter months. For this reason a full 12 months of Vital Sign data is used in Step Two for each moving average calculation; this gives a true and accurate picture of the strength (or weakness) of the market by way of the 12-month moving averages. This type of "apples and apples accounting" is most critical when you are analyzing the trend in existing home sales, which, as you will learn in the next two chapters, is usually the first Vital Sign indicator to signal future trend reversals.

Thirdly, the year-to-year comparisons for market momentum readings in Step Three are used because (1) they are keyed into the long-term nature of real estate trends, and (2) market research and testing prove that year-to-year comparisons for these key Vital Sign indicators allow you to accurately detect underlying market strength (or weakness) before it is reflected in actual real estate price trends. (In most cases, real estate prices tend to be a "lagging indicator" to trends in the Vital Sign indicators.)

Keep in mind that the market momentum readings compare Vital Sign moving averages for the most current month (call it "today") *against* Vital Sign moving averages in the recent past (a year ago from "today"). By seeing where these Vital Sign indicators *have been* as opposed to where they are *now*, you can tell which direction their trends are going and therefore the direction the market is likely to go.

Sources of Vital Sign Information

One of the biggest challenges you will face for tracking Vital Sign trends is collecting the actual data. This is true because the monthly statistics — with the exception of interest rates — are specific to a single major metropolitan area.

Remember, it is rare for any two U.S. real estate markets to move in tandem. An aerospace *boom* in Seattle, Washington can be driving property values higher. However, at the same time, a technology *bust* in San Jose, California can be causing real estate values to fall. In a like manner, changes in the broad U.S. economy — whether positive or negative — may also impact one region more significantly than another.

Because of the local nature of real estate trends, it is likely that you will have to obtain the relevant Vital Sign data for the city in which you live (or intend to buy or sell) from either state or local sources. There are, however, a few national market data providers — such as Data Quick Information Services — that may be able to give you the market data that you will need.

For major cities in California, for example, here are some sources for Vital Sign data:

Vital Sign #1: *Existing home sales.* These monthly statistics can be obtained from a wide variety of data sources: (1) local newspapers, (2) state real estate associations, (3) Title Insurance Companies, (4) Data Quick Information Services (www.DQNews.com), or (5) any real estate agent who is a member of the Multiple Listing Service. (See the K.I.S.S. method for tracking trends in Chapter 11, page 132.)

Vital Sign #2: *New home building permits.* In California, the Construction Industry Research Board publishes this data monthly. You can contact them by phone (818-841-8210) or go to their web site (www.CIRBData.com). The cost is around $250 per year to subscribe.

For major U.S. cities, building permit data can be found at these websites:

- U.S. Census Bureau
    http://censtats.census.gov/bldg/bldgprmt.shtml

- Texas A&M University
    www.recenter.tamu.edu/data/bpm/

Vital Sign #3: *Mortgage loan defaults.* These monthly statistics can be obtained from: (1) the County Recorder's Office, (2) newspapers that report legal notices, (3) Title Insurance Companies, and (4) Data Quick Information Services.

Vital Sign #4: *Foreclosure sales*: Same potential data sources as for Vital Sign #3.

Vital Sign #5: *Interest rates.* The data tracked for this key indicator is 30-year fixed rate mortgages. This can be found in any major financial newspaper such as (1) *The Wall Street Journal*, (2) *Investor's Business Daily*, or (3) *Barron's*.

This data can be also found on the website for the Federal Reserve Bank of St. Louis:

- *www.research.stlouisfed.org/fred2/*

Real Estate Timing is Like Horseshoes: You Can Win with Near Misses

Be clear about this: *real estate timing is not an exact science.* Without the benefit of incredible luck — or the market gods whispering buy/sell advice in your ear — you can't expect to buy at the *exact* market cycle lows and sell at the *exact* market cycle highs. The reason this is nearly impossible is due to the fact that peaks and bottoms in the real estate cycle do not occur at precise points in time when prices start to rise or fall. Instead, at major turning points in the cycles, real estate prices tend to level off for three to five months or so before the market distinctly starts trending in the other direction.

Because the Vital Sign indicators "lead the market," it is possible that you can buy within 5% of the market cycle lows and then sell within 5% of the market cycle highs. This allows you to profit from 90% (or more) of the entire market uptrend. And because real estate is normally purchased with a small down payment and a big loan from the bank — even with less than perfect real estate timing — the effects of leverage (borrowed money) can still provide you with spectacular profits that result from a rising market.

Here is an example. Let's say that you bought a $200,000 home with a 10% down payment right "near" the bottom of the market cycle. Then, four or five years later — near the peak — you sold the home for $320,000. While your home has appreciated 60% in value, your original $20,000 down payment has shot up to $120,000. While hindsight shows that you might have been able

Calculating Vital Sign Trends: Don't Sweat the Math

to pay a little less when you bought — and gotten a little more when you sold — you still have a 600% return on your money! When you have 90% of the purchase price leveraged with borrowed money, this shows how even near misses with market timing can still make you a consistent winner in real estate. Just like in horseshoes.

Words of Caution: Throw Away the Crystal Ball

Vital Sign momentum readings tell you when a major trend is starting and when it is ending. As good as they are for doing this, do not make the mistake of trying to extrapolate real estate trends too far into the future. This is fortune telling, not trend following.

For example, in predicting the weather, the best that even the most highly skilled meteorologists can do is predict three days in advance. Beyond that, accuracy becomes more guesswork than science. While real estate trends cannot be compared with weather trends, the point to be made is that the short-term is always more certain than the long-term. This is true of everything in life; you have a much better idea what is going to happen during the next three months than you do the next three years. Thus, even though real estate trends generally go for three to five years in each direction, this is only a rough rule of thumb. Trends can change at any time — this year's boom can be next year's bust.

It is for this reason that long-term economic forecasts are consistently off the mark. As with long-term weather forecasts, by extrapolating present-day economic trends into the distant future, long-term economic forecasts are doomed to failure from the start. To make a forecast, the only thing an economist can do is mathematically extend and project what is happening today into the future. They cannot take into account changes in market conditions, changes in technology, or anything else that can unexpectedly alter conditions. This is why these one, two or five-year forecasts are never right except by accident. Hence the saying: "If you have to forecast, forecast often."

Demand: The Driving Force behind Real Estate Trends

Real estate trends are driven by fundamental changes in demand, that is, changes that develop *before* prices actually change direction. However, the general public rarely digs deeper into the "economic facts" that drive these fundamentals, and instead are guilty of looking at the market from a superficial basis by focusing almost solely on prices. In so doing, this puts the public behind the curve — not ahead of it — because real estate prices tend to lag — not lead — changes in demand.

The important point to be made is that while no one knows for sure exactly how the future is going to unfold, the trends that move us there are measurable and identifiable with the Vital Sign indicators.

When demand is high at market cycle peaks, there is a shortage of properties. This is the best time to sell. When demand is low at market cycle bottoms, there is a shortage of cash. This is the best time to buy. As you will see in the next two chapters, Vital Sign charts tell you when these events are occurring.

– Chapter 7 –

The Best Time to Buy: A Vital Signs Case Study

*The best time to buy is when the
blood is running in the streets.*
— Nathan M. Rothchild

Rothchild's statement is as true today as when it was made in 1883. Buying during periods of doom and gloom — when the market is depressed — can always yield the greatest profits. Periods of maximum uncertainty are usually periods of maximum opportunity. If you apply J. Paul Getty's contrarian formula from Chapter 5, this is the best time to buy real estate: it is when demand, and therefore prices, are likely to be at their low point in the market cycle.

This chapter will show how the Vital Sign indicators signaled a tremendous buying opportunity for San Diego real estate in late 1996. After prices had declined by 30-40% from 1990 to 1996, these Vital Sign buying signals occurred when the public still had gloomy and negative expectations for the future.

Why was the public's mood so pessimistic? From the previous market cycle peak in 1989, the 1990's San Diego real estate market went into a severe downturn. Existing home sales fell by 55%, new home building permits fell by 85%, Notice of Defaults rose by

190%, and foreclosure sales rose by 600%. Yes, there was blood in the streets!

J. Paul Getty's contrarian formula works in all markets — including real estate — because human nature never changes: people are greedy when they should be afraid, and fearful when they should be actively looking to buy. In the stock market, for example, economic recessions have consistently presented investors with great opportunities to buy stock. This is illustrated in Chart 7-6, found in the Appendix.

Distinguishing Characteristics of Market Cycle Bottoms

The better you recognize market conditions that exist during *Stage One* market cycle bottoms, the better that you can anticipate Vital Sign signals to buy. Here are the telltale characteristics that identify a low point in the real estate cycle:

- Real estate is perceived to be a high-risk investment. Even though prices are depressed, the expectation is that prices are still going lower.

- Home sale activity is at multi-year lows. There are few buyers and few sellers.

- Construction activity is way down. New home building permits are at multi-year lows. Many builders have left the business or have gone bankrupt.

- The economy is sluggish or severely depressed. Unemployment is high and still rising. Incomes are at their lowest level. Job security is low.

- Mortgage financing is more difficult to get. Banks have a lot of bad loans and own many foreclosed properties.

- The media is reporting stories of doom and gloom.

- Consumer confidence is low as a pessimistic outlook hangs over the market and future expectations. The word on the street is: "Real estate is a bad investment. It is going to take a long time before prices rise again."

No price is too low for real estate pessimists. Nevertheless, with market negativity running high, property values depressed, and the media full of dismal news, the stage is set for the next real estate uptrend. Prices will soon start to rise like a phoenix from the cinders of recession. As a real estate contrarian that is watching the Vital Sign indicators, you are in the catbird seat, licking your lips and ready to pounce.

Vital Sign Signals to Buy:
A 1990's Case Study for San Diego, California

Real estate bottoms are not made with a roar, but a whimper. They occur at a time of low home sale activity, when just about everybody who wants to sell has done so. With few sellers, almost any increase in buying activity (increased demand) will start to send real estate prices higher.

Between 1990 and 1996, during which San Diego real estate prices fell by 30-40%, the Vital Sign indicators signaled the emergence of a new market uptrend. The result was that home prices rose by roughly 70-100% from late 1996 until early 2002.

As explained in Chapter 3, there is a sequence in which you can expect the Vital Sign indicators to give trend change signals. Signal by signal, Charts 7-1 to 7-5 show you the order in which these key indicators heralded the beginning of a new market upcycle for the San Diego real estate prices.

The first signal to buy was given by Vital Sign #1: *existing home sales*. As shown in Chart 7-1 on the next page, this signal occurred in March 1996, when the market momentum reading climbed from below the "0" line to above the "0" line. This crossing of the "0" line indicated that a trend change in existing home sales had occurred, changing from a downtrend into an uptrend. This was a positive sign for the San Diego real estate market because increasing demand generally means increasing property values.

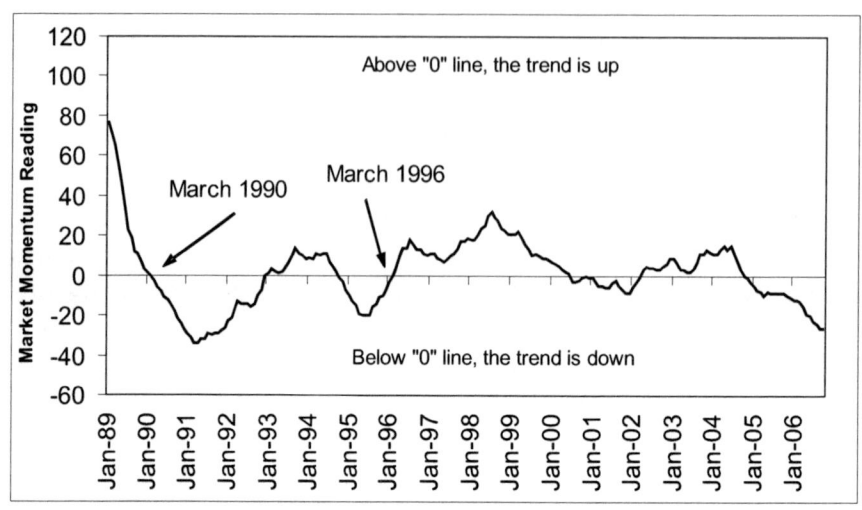

Chart 7-1: Vital Sign #1
Existing Home Sales
San Diego, California 1989–2006

(Refer to Appendix for Chart 7-1 market momentum calculations.)

The second signal to buy was given by Vital Sign #2: *new home building permits*. As shown in Chart 7-2, this signal occurred in

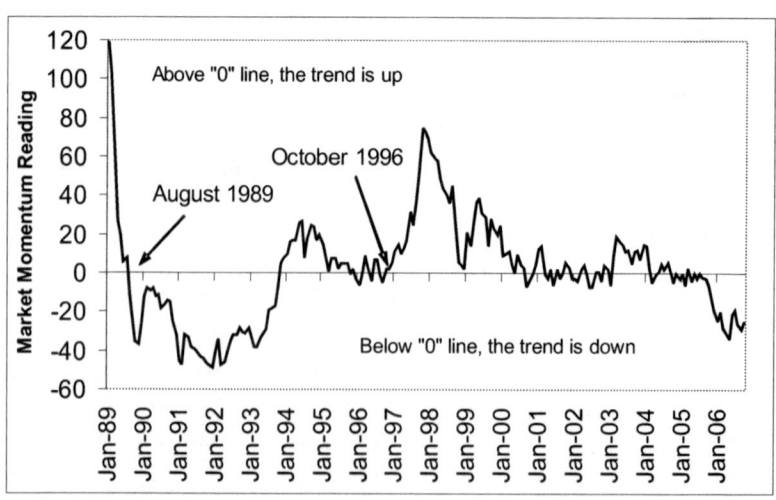

Chart 7-2: Vital Sign #2
New Home Building Permits
San Diego, California 1989–2006

October 1996, when the market momentum reading climbed from below the "0" line to above it. This crossing of the "0" line signaled that the trend in new home building permits had changed from a downtrend into an uptrend. This was a positive sign for the market because it showed that there was an increasing demand for new homes to be built.

Notice how the momentum readings for new home building permits moved slightly above and below the "0" line three times prior to that final signal in October 1996. This is why multiple Vital Sign signals are recommended before you make buying or selling decisions.

(Refer to Appendix for Chart 7-2 market momentum calculations.)

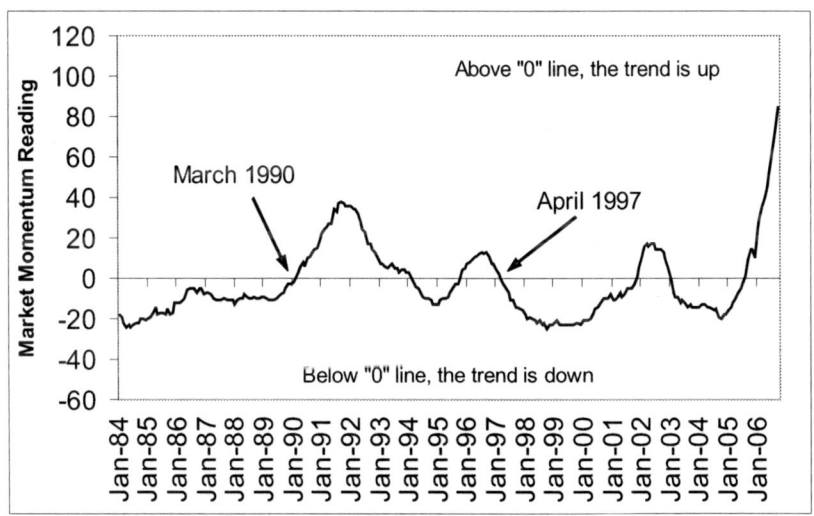

Chart 7-3: Vital Sign #3
Mortgage Loan Defaults
San Diego, California 1989–2006

The third signal to buy was given by Vital Sign #3: *mortgage loan defaults*. As shown in Chart 7-3, this signal occurred in April 1997, when the market momentum reading fell from above the "0" line to below the "0" line. This crossing of the "0" line signaled that the trend in mortgage loan defaults had changed from an uptrend to a downtrend. With fewer and fewer homeowners having difficulty making their mortgage payments, this was a positive sign for the San Diego economy and its real estate market.

Note the Vital Sign domino effect: when you see that Vital Signs #1, #2, and #3 all give signals to buy, you can now be 80-90% confident that a major real estate upcycle is underway.

(Refer to Appendix for Chart 7-3 market momentum calculations.)

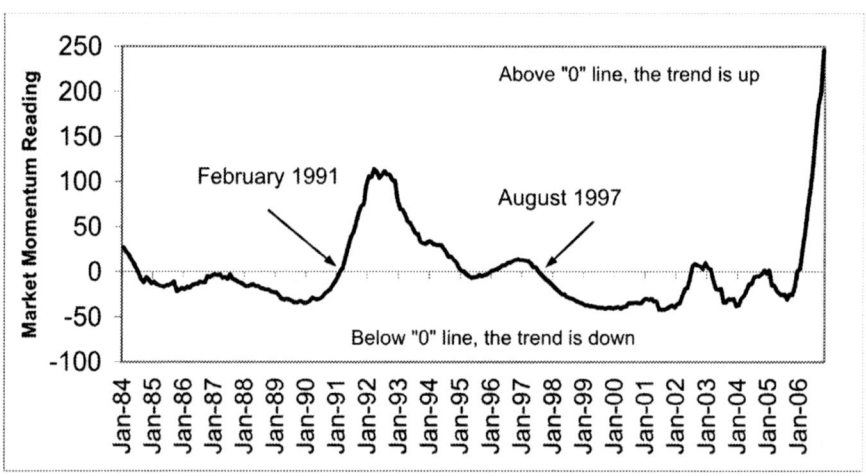

Chart 7-4: Vital Sign #4
Foreclosure Sales
San Diego, California 1989–2006

The fourth signal to buy was given by Vital Sign #4: *foreclosure sales*. As shown in Chart 7-4, this signal occurred in August 1997, when the market momentum reading fell from above the "0" line to below the "0" line. When the "0" line was crossed, this signaled the trend in foreclosure sales had changed from an uptrend to a downtrend. With fewer and fewer foreclosure sales, this was a positive sign for the market. Just like the downtrend in mortgage loan defaults, this showed that the San Diego economy was getting stronger.

(Refer to Appendix for Chart 7-4 market momentum calculations.)

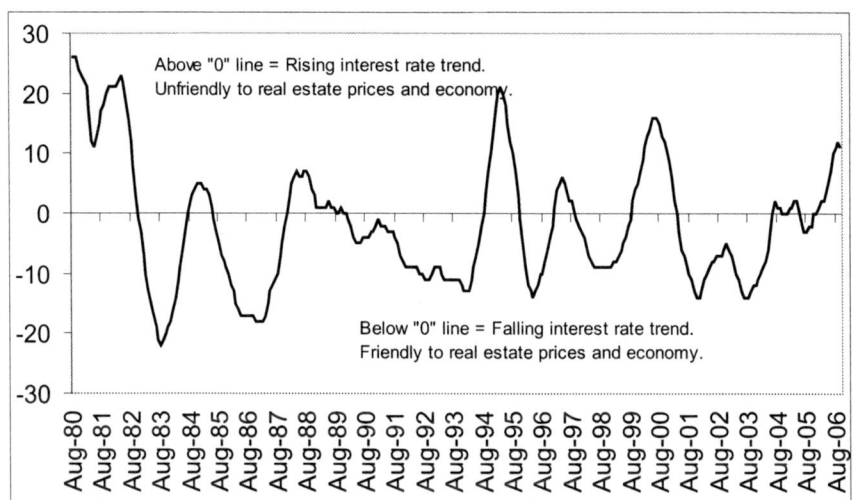

Chart 7-5: Vital Sign #5
Interest Rates
San Diego, California 1980–2006

Vital Sign indicator #5, *interest rates*, is shown in Chart 7-5. As you know from Chapter 4, *The Campbell Method* uses trends in interest rates not as a key predictor of real estate trends, but to indicate when the prevailing trend of the market is likely to get stronger or weaker. For example, the market momentum reading fell from above the "0" line to below the "0" line in October 1997. This signaled that interest rates were trending down, which is a good sign for the real estate market.

(Refer to Appendix for Chart 7-5 market momentum calculations.)

Buy Early and Ride the Trend Higher

As explained in Chapter 6, the Vital Sign indicators do not try to predict the distant future — but they do help you anticipate the movement of trends before everyone else does. Clearly, the best time to buy anything is early, before increasing demand starts to move prices significantly higher. Then once it *does* becomes obvious that a new real estate uptrend is underway, you can ride the trend higher until the market peaks. Then you sell.

Staying a step or two ahead of the crowd is the goal of *The Campbell Method*.

In early 1997, which was about six to 12 months after Vital Signs #1 through #3 gave "buy signals" for the San Diego real estate market, property values started an impressive climb to higher and higher levels. On April 26, 1998, the following headline appeared on the front page of the *San Diego Union-Tribune*: "Homebuyers, beware: It's a sellers' market."

Be clear about this: rising real estate prices *do* attract attention. They also attract more and more buyers who want to own a home and make money. This means that rising real estate markets pick up more and more upward momentum as time goes on. This is why you want to buy early. And it also explains why the greatest gains in price appreciation generally occur in the last one to two years of the market upcycle. Fueled by greed, this is when "irrational exuberance" takes over and the greatest number of the general public rush into the market to buy, causing a final upward "spike" in prices right before upward momentum starts to slow and the market reaches its peak.

As real estate prices rise higher, you may be tempted to sell too early before the market peaks — for a smaller profit — and thus enjoy more *immediate gratification*. If possible, try to avoid doing this. Although there is an old adage that says "you never go broke making a small profit," this is not the best way to get rich. Don't be satisfied with a small profit in real estate — strive for a maximum profit. Ride the trend until it ends.

Warning! Beware of Buying Late

"What the wise do early, the foolish do late" is an axiom in all markets.

The biggest mistake that you can make in real estate is buying near a market peak. However this is what a great number of homebuyers do because they are lured into overpriced markets late, like moths to a bright light. This is evidenced by the fact that there are an ever-increasing number of home sales that occur during each advancing year of a market upcycle. Like Mr. and Mrs. Armstrong in Chapter 2, a huge number of homebuyers who "buy late" put themselves at serious economic risk when the trend turns down and prices fall.

Rental properties — both large and small — can be particularly vulnerable during a market downcycle. And if you buy near a market peak — or early into a market downcycle — the risks become even greater.

Contrary to a popular misconception, rarely is it the case that when the market for home sales gets worse, the market for rentals gets better. The fact is, local real estate markets tend to move in lockstep with the local economy and job market. Thus, when the real estate market turns down, the economy turns down, jobs disappear, and people are forced to move elsewhere to find employment, vacating rental properties.

Bottom line: Rents tend to fall — and vacancies tend to rise — during real estate downturns. This unfavorable set of circumstances — especially when combined with a large mortgage payment — can result in a significant negative cash flow for real estate investors. Furthermore, a bad market can last longer than your bank account. If this happens — if you run out of cash reserves to meet expenses — you can be forced to sell at a time when property values are depressed and there are few buyers.

In high-priced markets that exist in California, where the price of housing is double the national average, the name of the real estate game is *appreciation* — not rental cash flow. Unless you are willing to put a 30-40% down payment on the purchase of a one-to-four unit rental property — which few investors do — you can expect a negative cash flow.

Exception to Real Estate Timing Rules

There *is* an exception to this "buy at the market cycle bottom" timing strategy.

While it is never prudent to buy right after a market peak, when home prices are still highly inflated, it can be okay to buy after a market downtrend has been underway for a year or two *if* you can buy at 20-30% below market value. This is called making a profit "going into the deal." And even though you are going against the trend — which is generally risky and unadvisable — buying real estate at a huge discount to current market value *can* give you a significant "margin of safety" if prices continue to move lower.

From a practical standpoint, it is difficult to buy property at 20-30% below market value. Real estate "super bargains" are very rare and normally require huge amounts of time, persistence, and energy to locate. To find these profitable deals, you often must be prepared to look at 50 to 100 properties — and then make 10 to 20 purchase offers. This Herculean effort can make real estate bargain hunting a full time occupation — and most people are simply not up to the task.

If you can't buy at least 20-30% below market during a real estate decline — and this is a key point to managing risk — the safe approach is to wait until the Vital Sign indicators give you signals to buy.

Better Safe than Sorry

As valuable as the Vital Sign indicators are for identifying trends, they are not an exact science. Occasionally the market doesn't do what these indicators say it should do. For example, let's say the Vital Sign indicators tell you that the trend is down — but property values remain firm and don't seem to want to fall from their previous peak.

Does this mean it is safe to buy?

Maybe . . . but maybe not. From a risk/reward standpoint, if the Vital Sign indicators say "sell," the odds of prices moving lower are high . . . not low.

Equally risky, how do you know whether a real estate downturn is going to stay mild or nosedive into a significant drop? That is a tough question, and if someone tells you that they know the answer, they are kidding both you and themselves.

When the Vital Sign indicators say that the trend is down, it is better to be certain you will avoid a market downtrend than be hopeful that one doesn't materialize. Because real estate is an illiquid asset (hard to sell) you would rather be out of the market wanting in, than in the market wanting out.

From a risk management standpoint, focus on the market — not the money. If you stay aligned with the trend, only good things can happen. For this reason, it is usually safer to pay 5% *more* for a home when you know the trend is up than it is buying today (for less) when you know the trend is down.

Remember, if you manage risk correctly — if you do everything possible to avoid market downtrends — you will automatically be doing what you need to do to maximize profits. This is what successful real estate investment is all about.

Want to be Famous?

Andy Warhol once predicted: "In the future, everyone will be famous for 15 minutes." To be famous (and rich) in real estate, when opportunity knocks, buy something. If you don't own the home you live in, buy one. If you already own a home, buy a rental property. If you're an investor who already owns rental properties, buy more.

Real estate ownership has created more millionaires than any other type of investment. Trying to keep the market down is like trying to hold a beach ball under water. Sooner or later, the market will start to trend higher again, usually taking prices to new all-time highs.

Remember, real estate timing is not about buying a home at what you "think" is a good time — or at what you "think" is a cheap price when the chances of the market rising higher in the very near future are only so-so. This approach is like betting on a spin of the roulette wheel. Instead, you want to use *The Campbell Method* to buy a home not only when prices are low . . . but also at a time when probability is high that home prices will appreciate almost immediately.

You don't have to be a math whiz to understand that even small improvements in real estate timing can produce massive increases in your results. As you have learned in this chapter, when you can anticipate that a trend is going to change, buying early is always better than buying late.

As you will learn in the next chapter, the same guideline applies to exiting the market. When the Vital Signs say the market is peaking, selling early is always better than selling late.

– Chapter 8 –

The Best Time to Sell: A Vital Signs Case Study

Plan ahead: It wasn't raining when Noah built the Ark.
— Richard Cushing

"You should have sold last year" are the six words that real estate owners hate to hear.

The best-kept secret in real estate isn't what to buy . . . or even when to buy. The greatest secret is knowing when to sell. While we all like to talk about the great success stories that result in tremendous upside profits, never forget that there is always a downside lurking as well.

If your goal is to maximize profits, then once you buy a property — whether it's a home you live in or a rental property — your entire focus must shift to the only thing that is within your control: knowing when to sell for the highest price. Interestingly, however, if you look at all of those hundreds of "how-to" books on making money in real estate, not one book ever tells you when to sell. They always talk about buying. But whether you own a piece of real estate for three years or 30 years, how do you maximize profits if you don't know what the best time to sell is?

In any event, protecting capital is the first rule of money. To do this, you can't just buy and hope. Never buy anything unless you know under what conditions you will sell it.

Selling High When the Market is Peaking

"Take care to sell your horse before he dies. The art of living is passing losses on," advised Robert Frost.

When a real estate uptrend dies, there are good reasons to sell your home or rental property. For one, in times of economic change, there are always transfers of wealth. Clearly, those who sell at a market peak win. Those who buy from them lose. And those who hold on — and do not sell — lose more than the time value of money by having to wait for the market to recover to its previous peak. By failing to take profits when prices were high, those who don't sell also lose the golden opportunity to buy again at lower prices.

Another reason to take profits near the peak is that real estate is an "illiquid" asset, and not easily converted into cash. Even when homes sales are setting record highs and prices are rising, it can still take time and serious effort to find a buyer. This is because, unlike selling, buying a home is a purely discretionary activity. Thus, selling into a strong market — where there is a lot of demand — is not only the way to maximize profits; it is also the easiest time to sell a piece of property. Conversely, when demand falls during a real estate downturn, competition for buyers gets more and more intense. This is *not* the time that you want to be selling.

As they say in the jungle, when you are waist deep in alligators, it is too late to ask why someone didn't drain the swamp. In real estate, when you read the headline "Real Estate Prices are Plunging," it is too late to ask why someone didn't advise you to sell.

In order to be successful in real estate, it is up to you to use *The Campbell Method* to anticipate future headlines. This doesn't mean that you should be able to guess what next month's–or next year's — Vital Sign data will be. Nobody can do that. But it does mean that you need to intelligently monitor today's economic events — *and* Vital Sign data — that provide you with a preview of what is to come.

Distinguishing Characteristics of Real Estate Peaks

The better that you recognize market conditions that exist during *Stage Three* market cycle peaks (page 19), the better you can anticipate Vital Sign signals to sell. Here are the telltale characteristics that identify a peak in the real estate cycle:

- Real estate is perceived to be almost risk-free. Prices are extremely high, yet everyone expects property values to continue to rise.

- Home sale activity is at (or near) multi-year highs. There are many buyers and many sellers.

- New home construction is at (or near) multi-year highs. There are a large number of homebuilders in the business.

- The economy is strong, maybe even booming. Unemployment is low and continuing to fall. Job security is high. Incomes are at their highest level.

- Mortgage financing is easy to obtain. As a general rule, if you pass the "fog the mirror" test, you qualify. The banks have few bad loans and even fewer foreclosed properties that they must try to sell.

- The media is reporting on how terrific everything is — for both the economy and the real estate market.

- Extreme optimism rules the market and future expectations. Consumer confidence is high. The word on the street is: "Even though real estate prices are high, they won't go down. There is a shortage of housing." (Translation: "There is no need to sell. It's different this time.")

The final stages of a real estate boom — and the market downturn that is likely to follow — occur in an atmosphere of extreme optimism, even euphoria. After a long and significant rise in home prices– where making money is easy–irrational exuberance takes over. At this point, everybody starts to believe property values can only go one way . . . higher.

But real estate is most dangerous when it looks the easiest. When almost all people are crowded into one side of public opinion, when everyone seems to believe that real estate is a risk-free investment, the law of contrary thinking dictates that it is time to take the other side and sell.

Vital Sign Signals to Sell:
A 1989 Case Study for San Diego, California

The following case study shows how the 1989 Vital Sign indicators gave "advance warning" to the 1990's San Diego real estate crash. After rising by 100-150% during the boom of the 1980's, property values fell by 30-40% during the next six years. The sell signals turned out to be far more than a temporary death sentence for price appreciation. Before it was over, this bust in the San Diego real estate market had destroyed more wealth than anything since the Great Depression.

Signal by signal, here is the sequence in which the Vital Sign indictors heralded the beginning of a new market downcycle for San Diego real estate prices in early 1990.

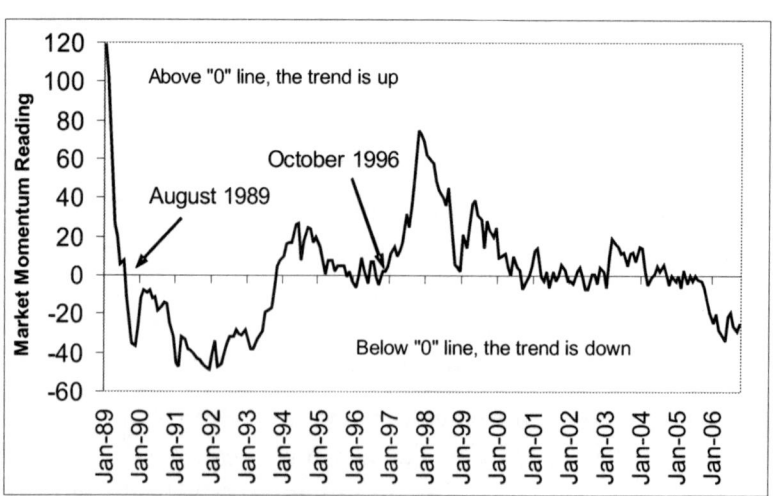

Chart 8-1: Vital Sign #2
New Home Buildling Permits
San Diego, California, 1989-2006

The Best Time to Sell: A Vital Signs Case Study

The first signal to sell was given by Vital Sign #2: *new home building permits*. As shown in Chart 8-1, this signal occurred in August 1989, when the market momentum reading fell from above the "0" line to below the "0" line. This crossing of the "0" line indicated a trend change in new home building permits had occurred — changing from an uptrend to a downtrend. This was a negative sign for the San Diego real estate market because it showed that there was decreasing demand for new homes being built.

(Refer to Appendix for Chart 8-1 market momentum calculations.)

The second signal to sell was given by Vital Sign #3: *mortgage loan defaults*. As shown in Chart 8-2, this signal occurred in March 1990, when the market momentum reading climbed from below the "0" line to above the "0" line. When the "0" line was crossed, this signaled that the trend in foreclosure sales had changed from a downtrend to an uptrend. With more and more homeowners having difficulty making their mortgage payments,

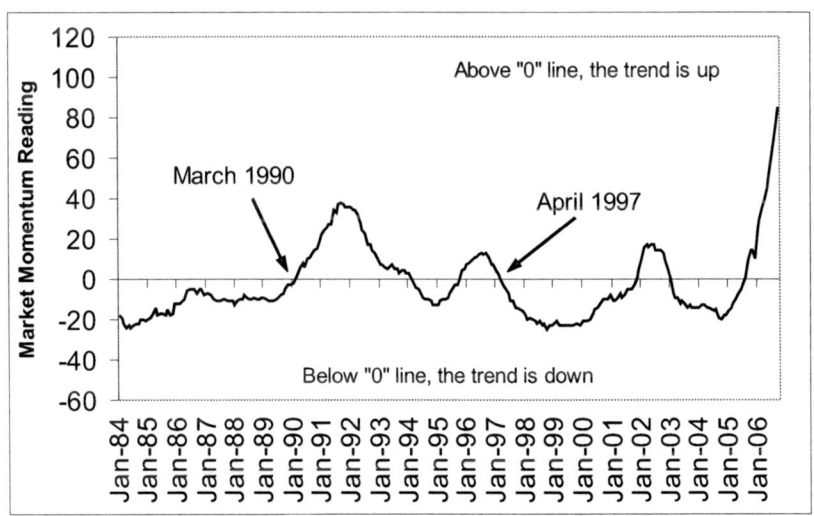

Chart 8-2: Vital Sign #3
New Home Building Permits
San Diego, California, 1984-2006

this was a negative sign for the San Diego economy and its real estate market.

(Refer to Appendix for Chart 8-2 market momentum calculations.)

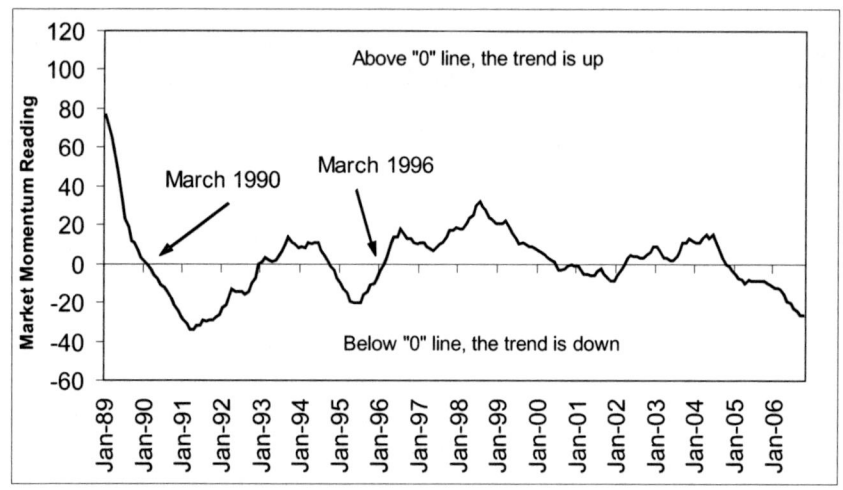

Chart 8-3: Vital Sign #1
Existing Home Sales
San Diego, California, 1989-2006

The third signal to sell was given by Vital Sign #1: *existing home sales*. As shown in Chart 8-3, this signal occurred in March 1990, when the market momentum reading fell from above the "0" line to below it. This crossing of the "0" line signaled the trend in existing home sales had changed from an uptrend into a downtrend. This is a negative sign for the San Diego real estate market because it shows that home buying demand was decreasing.

Note the Vital Sign domino effect: when you see that Vital Signs #1, #2, and #3 all give signals to sell, you can now be 80-90% confident that a major real estate downcycle is underway.

(Refer to Appendix for Chart 8-3 market momentum calculations.)

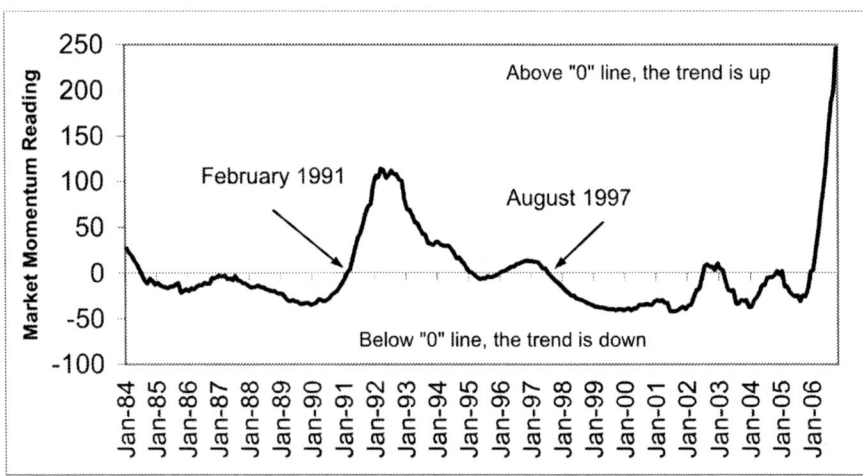

Chart 8-4: Vital Sign #4
Foreclosure Sales
San Diego, California, 1989-2006

The fourth signal to sell was given by Vital Sign #4: *foreclosure sales*. As shown on Chart 8-4, this signal occurred in February 1991, when the market momentum reading climbed from below the "0" line to above the "0" line. When the "0" line was crossed, this signaled the trend in foreclosure sales had changed from a downtrend to an uptrend. With more and more foreclosure sales, this was a negative sign for the market. Just like the uptrend that occurred in mortgage loan defaults, this showed that the San Diego economy was getting weaker.

Notice that this sell signal occurred between 13 and 18 months *after* the sell signals from Vital Signs #1 through #3. While this offered even more persuasive evidence that San Diego real estate prices were indeed heading lower, recall that foreclosure sales tend to be a "lagging indicator" at market peaks. This means that real estate prices will likely turn lower *before* this indicator crosses the "0" line, which will be after the time you should have sold.

(Refer to Appendix for Chart 8-4 market momentum calculations.)

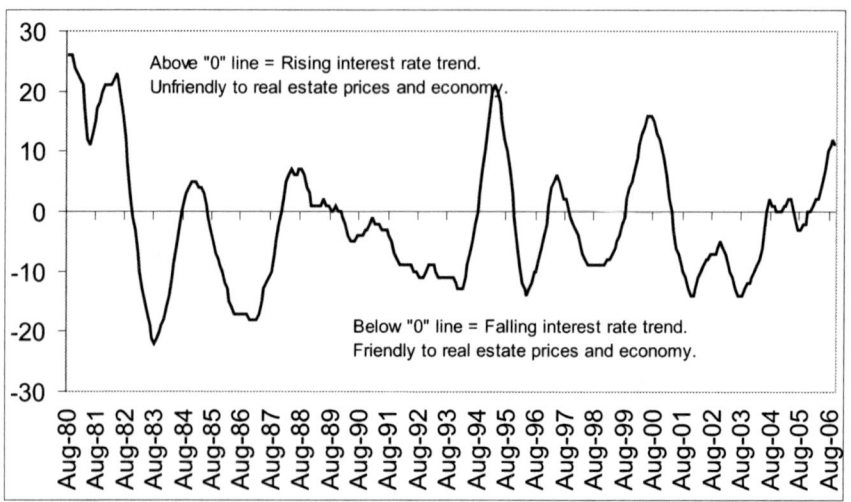

Chart 8-5: Vital Sign #5
Interest Rates
San Diego, California, 1980-2006

Vital Sign indicator #5: *interest rates*, is shown in Chart 8-5. As you know from Chapter 4, *The Campbell Method* does not use interest rates as a key predictor of real estate trends, but as an indicator of when the prevailing trend of the market is likely to get stronger or weaker.

Interestingly, beginning in January 1990–and through most of the 1990's downtrend for the San Diego real estate market — the trend in interest rates was also down! This showed that–by itself–falling interest rates were unable to jump-start demand and prevent prices from spiraling down.

"Cheaper Loans Fail to Revive Home Sales" was the *L.A. Times* headline on February 7, 1991. As is often the case, there are always other market forces at work whose effects (either positive or negative) can obscure the effect that interest rate trends have on real estate prices. But consider this: if interest rates had been rising during the first half of the 1990's, it is likely that the San Diego real estate decline would have been even more severe.

(Refer to Appendix for Chart 8-5 market momentum calculations.)

The news media was having a hay-day because bad news is always a big seller. With rare exception, California real estate prices (not only San Diego prices) were in a free-fall and the whole nation was watching with interest. "Housing Cave-In: Home Prices Fall, Rattling Southern California" reported *The Wall Street Journal* in October 1992.

Look at the broad sampling of newspaper headlines from the *San Diego Union-Tribune* and the *L.A. Times* from 1991 to 1994:

A Word (Again) About The Experts

Did any of the experts predict the San Diego real estate downturn? As far as this writer knows, there were none. This reaffirms the fact that, prior to *The Campbell Method*, determining the best times to buy and real estate has essentially been a "do-it-yourself" project.

While the experts failed to predict the market peak, many were certain that they could predict the market bottom. "Buy Now, Experts Urge," was the March 1991 headline in the *San Diego*

Union Tribune. Reading further, the article said: "Soft housing market not expected to last long. There has rarely been a better time to buy." Because the downtrend would last until 1996, the advice from these modern day soothsayers proved — once again — to be way off the mark.

The Rise and Fall of Real Estate Prices: Statistics Can be Deceiving

Here's a pop quiz: The price of your home rises by 80% during a five-year uptrend — and then falls by 30% during the subsequent three-year downtrend.

At the end of the eighth year, by what percentage are you ahead?

If you answer 50% (80% minus 30%), you aren't even close.

The correct answer is 26%.

Here is how to do the calculations. Let's say that you buy a home for $100,000 at a market cycle bottom. After it appreciates by 80%, the home is now worth $180,000 at the market peak. From the market peak, the home now depreciates by 30%, causing it to lose $54,000 of its previous value (30% x $180,000). Thus, after eight years of ownership, the value of your home at the market bottom is $126,000, which is 26% more than you originally paid.

This is why appreciation and depreciation statistics can easily deceive people. But was your home still a good investment? Sure. Even though you didn't sell at the market peak — where you could have netted an $80,000 profit — you did buy at the previous market bottom. This means that at the end of eight years, you made a $26,000 "paper profit" from a $10,000 original investment, which was your down payment. This gives you a total eight-year return of 260% ($26,000 divided by $10,000) or an annual rate of return of 32.5 % per year (260% divided by eight years).

To show how market downtrends destroy wealth faster than market uptrends create it — and why real estate timing is important — let's consider another example. This time, however, let's assume that you didn't buy your home for $100,000 at the market cycle bottom. Instead, you paid $126,000 for it two years later, after the market had already moved higher. At the market peak, your home is still worth $180,000, giving you a paper profit of $54,000 because it appreciated by 43% during three years. Again, you don't sell — and three years later the ensuing 30% decline (though smaller than the 43% rise) would ultimately wipe out *all* of your profit. After six years, the home you paid $126,000 for is again worth $126,000. Thus, your $10,000 down payment is again worth $10,000 six years later. Adjusted for inflation, you lose money on this investment.

Knowing when to sell is more important than knowing when to buy. From a return-on-investment standpoint, price appreciation is measured from the market bottom and price depreciation is measured from the market peak. In other words, you can buy at almost any time during a market upcycle and make money. But you can't sell anytime and make money. This is why *The Campbell Method* places "knowing when to sell" — the greatest secret in real estate — at the pinnacle of decision-making.

Protecting Your Money: You Have a Lot to Lose

A home may be where the heart is, but it is also where your net worth is. After years of appreciation, most Americans have a lot of money to protect.

The important question, then, is always the same: What happens next? Are property values going to continue to shoot up, making homeowners more and more rich? Or is a serious real estate downturn lying in wait like a burglar, ready to steal your profits? While no one knows for sure, we do know this: the decision to sell at a market peak may turn out to be a minor mistake; the decision not to sell can turn out to be a major disaster.

There is nothing wrong with being a fair-weather fan. Just as a smart general does not keep his troops in battle all the time, a smart individual does not keep his money in real estate all the time. Cash is an investment too. When real estate prices are falling — your cash is appreciating. And when the Vital Signs tell you that the market downturn is over, you will be in the perfect position to "buy low" while those around you will not.

Looking Ahead to Avoid Trouble

The importance of knowing when to sell is illustrated by a story about a very rich man who made millions in real estate, adding to his fortune during both good times *and* bad. Growing up poor in Chicago, this young boy had an experience that prepared him well for adjusting to changing market conditions.

Returning home from school one day, dirty and with a bloody nose from a fight, the boy walked into the tenement where his mom was mopping the floor. "What happened to you?" she asked.

"I was beat up by those two bullies down the street," he answered. With little sympathy, his mother took her wet mop and swatted him across the face.

Startled but unhurt, he asked: "What is that for?"

"That's for getting in their way!" his mom shot back.

Rising real estate markets are what make you rich. Avoiding bad markets is what keeps you rich. While this lesson about *learning how to avoid trouble* might have been taught more gently, it had a lasting effect on the young boy. It made him rich because he knew when to get out of the way of bad markets.

In the next chapter, you will learn *The Campbell Method's* "Three Market Truths," which teach you to respect what the ultimate real estate " guru — the market itself — is telling you to do. Follow these truths and you will prosper — ignore them and you are putting your money at unnecessary risk.

– Chapter 9 –

The Campbell Method: Three Market Truths

The trouble with man is twofold. He cannot learn truths that are too complicated: he forgets truths that are too simple.
— Rebecca West

In real estate, success is never certain. No trend goes on forever. Money has to be actively managed. Money has to be moved.

With the impact that technology has had in reshaping society — how we work and where we live — today's economic events are changing things faster than ever. And even with a continued rising tide of national prosperity, the areas of local prosperity will change — causing some areas to prosper and others to decline. Thus, as areas of economic opportunity shift, so will trends in real estate prices.

And if you strip away all explanations and theories about how to stay ahead of the market trends, you will discover some simple, yet timeless, truths that will reward you with the greatest financial yields. Woven into *The Campbell Method*, these truths are not idealistic or difficult to understand. They do not leave you "up in the air," not knowing what to do. Instead, they are realistic, practical and very definite for determining the best times to buy and sell.

Market Truth #1: The Vital Signs are the language of the real state market. When they talk, listen.

Market Truth #2: Trust what you see, not what you think.

Market Truth #3: The market is always right, you aren't.

There is only one reason why you don't achieve your maximum profit potential in real estate: the trend of the market changes and you don't. These three market truths can help you recognize why this happens . . . and what you can do to correct the problem.

**Market Truth #1:
The Vital Signs are the Language of the Real Estate Market.
When They Talk, Listen.**

"Good intelligence is nine-tenths of any battle," Napoleon would counsel his generals. In the markets, the battle is won with good information as well.

To secure this advantage in real estate, the best and most reliable source of trend information does not come from the experts or newspaper headlines. Instead, the source is the market itself — and by following certain key indicators that have proven themselves to be highly correlated with price movement, the market speaks to you in a language that clearly reveals its future intentions.

The Vital Sign Charts Tell All

If pictures are worth a thousand words, Vital Sign charts are worth a thousand economic forecasts. This is because markets are people and — at any point in time — the way in which the collective market is reacting to economic events, to government events, and to rumors and other news is *all* reflected in the movement of these indicators.

As such, these Vital Sign charts are simply a graphic representation of supply and demand in action, giving you a true and accurate "bottom line" accounting of all the hopes, fears and greed that are always swirling in the marketplace. That is why these charts "tell all." Thus, when the prevailing trend is going to change direction — either up or down, and for whatever the reasons — you are going to know about it.

In essence, the Vital Sign indicators can be looked upon as the market's messengers of truth. Unlike the economists who use "intellectual guesswork" to try to predict the future, these indicators are a direct reflection of reality . . . and do not speculate on the unknown and unknowable. They take much of the risk out of intelligent decision-making. You can make decisions — such as buy, sell or hold tight — based on what the market *is* doing, as opposed to what the market *might* do.

Be clear about this: the Vital Sign indicators are *not* a "magic formula" for guaranteed riches in real estate. Nobody will ever have all the details about where the markets are going. Nevertheless, when the trends are going to change — which they always do — the odds are heavy that these Vital Sign indicators will "speak" with strong conviction. And when this happens, as research has proven, you are wise to believe it.

Listen to the market, it will tell you what it wants to do.

Market Truth #2:
Trust What You See, Not What You Think

"The world is round," declared Christopher Columbus.

"That's crazy," the public said. "It is flat."

To prove his point, Columbus offered a simple, yet convincing, argument. When sailors were at sea and another ship was coming towards them, they would first see the mast, then the sails, and then finally the hull would come into view.

"The world can't be flat," reasoned Columbus, "otherwise the entire ship would become visible all at once."

The public was then convinced. They had evidence that could be verified by direct observation.

The moral of the story: you can believe what you see.

Don't Think, Look

Like Christopher Columbus proved to us centuries earlier, you can trust your eyes. And so it is in real estate. To make the best buying and selling decisions, the market has to be observed directly.

When you observe the real estate market directly, what you "see" — which is what the Vital Sign indicators and charts are telling you — is visual evidence about what is actually *happening* in the market. This is factual market data. And now that you know the relationship between this market data and future price trends, you can act upon this information with a high level of confidence.

What you "think" is happening in the market *can be* completely different from what you can "see." Most of the time, what you *think* is merely an "opinion," a personal viewpoint and nothing more. Even worse, in most cases our opinions are influenced by what we hope and want to happen in the market. In other words, *we see what we want to see* . . . instead of seeing what the market is actually showing.

Nevertheless, even though market opinions can differ greatly from market realities, everyone has them. You have them, your friends have them, real estate agents have them and the market experts make their living by having them. In fact, after you read or hear something, it is human nature to form opinions about what you *think* the market is going to do.

If you can't put a stop to having opinions, you must therefore do the next best thing before acting on them: make the market *confirm* that opinion — and prove it to be right — before you make a decision. Thus, act on what you know to be true, not what you think, hope or want to be true.

Market Truth #3:
The Market is Always Right; You Aren't

Ego is the enemy of successful investment. What you need is objectivity.

The Campbell Method: Three Market Truths

Until you let go of the false idea that you — or anybody else — knows more than the market does, you will be building up your ego instead of your bank account. For example, let's say that you have a belief about what direction the market will go. Your belief is based on what you consider to be high-quality information and an excellent reasoning ability. This may all be well and good except for one detail: if the market doesn't share your belief, it doesn't matter how "right" you think you are.

In other words, you can't pretend to be smarter than the market if you want to make the most money. The market gives you clear signals about where it wants to go.

Ego, however, shifts the contest between you and the market into a more difficult arena — a contest between you and yourself. Nobody likes to be wrong. Thus, a rigid, ego-driven approach says: "Don't confuse me with the facts, my mind is made up." By contrast, a flexible, market-driven approach says: "This is what the market says, therefore this is what I do."

In the battle for real estate profits, you need to invest with the trend — and ignore the ego's need to show off its own brilliance.

Do You Want to be Rich or Right?

Don't take this personally . . . but what you believe — or what someone else believes — is irrelevant to correctly identifying the market's trend. What the market "believes" is the only thing that matters. This is because the market will always move prices in the direction of the greatest force. Therefore, when buyers are the greatest force — meaning buyers have the greater numbers *relative* to sellers — prices will rise. When sellers are the dominant force — meaning there are fewer buyers *relative* to the number of sellers — prices will fall.

This simple, mechanical principle of "cause" and "effect" will always rule the market — regardless of what anyone believes to the contrary. For example, you may buy a home because you *believe* home prices are cheap and can't go any lower. However, if market forces continue to drive home values lower, then the sellers are right (not the buyers) and you are the one losing money. On the other hand, if you sell because you *believe* home prices can't go any higher, yet prices still continue to climb, then the buyers are right (not the sellers) and you are the one who missed the opportunity to make a greater profit.

So here's the question to ask yourself: "Do you want to make money — or do you want to be right?" As a buyer or seller who is looking to capitalize on trends in the marketplace, you need to be market-centric . . . not egocentric.

Profit is the measure of right in the real estate market. For this reason, it is *only you* who can be wrong — the market never is.

The Ultimate Truth: You Are Dancing with a Gorilla

As the economy changes — and real estate markets follow suit — your future prosperity will revolve around being flexible, open-minded, and willing to go with the market's flow. In real estate, never forget that those individuals who get closest to the truth will be least surprised by the future. For this reason, good market information will likely be the best weapon used by anyone who wants to adjust to change and stay ahead of the pack.

The ultimate truth of real estate is that the market plays the music and you must learn to dance to it. It grants its greatest fortunes to those who best respect its wishes and stay in step with the trends. In California, where the trends (up and down) can be equally powerful in both directions, dancing with the market is like dancing with an eight-hundred-pound gorilla. If you are smart, you will allow the gorilla to lead and you follow. Only the foolish try to resist the greater force.

– Chapter 10 –

The Campbell Method: A Timing System with Ten Cardinal Rules

There are only two emotions in the market — hope and fear. The problem is, you hope when you should fear, and you fear when you should hope.
— Jesse Livermore

Why is it that the best time to buy — or to sell — was always last year?

The biggest reason is really quite simple: while it is true that everyone wants to make money in real estate, it is also true that very few have a *pre-planned, established game plan* for doing so. Even worse, without an established game plan to follow, the average person falls prey to headline news, popular opinion, and emotion at precisely the time when market conditions are clearly shifting in the opposite direction.

To avoid this problem — and to more fully capitalize on the best buy and sell points in market cycles — the third component part of *The Campbell Method* is a "Real Estate Profit System" . . . a system that is based on *Ten Cardinal Rules*. Here are the key characteristics that make this Real Estate Profit System a consistent and dependable way to take your buying and selling efforts to the highest levels of profitability:

- The system is as close to "automatic and mechanical" as possible. The signals to buy and sell are predetermined ahead of time and require a minimum need for subjective interpretation.

- By using the Vital Sign indicators to track market trends, the system takes everything into account that the market can do. When you know what the market is going to do — the system defines what you should do in response.

- Risk management and money management are built into the system. There are specific rules for maximizing profits from the rising markets and specific rules for minimizing loss during the falling markets.

- The system is logical and easy to understand. You don't need any formal training in economics or finance to know why it works.

It is a "system with rules" that replaces market uncertainty and confusion and with a clearer sense of order and self-confidence. The following *Ten Cardinal Rules* tell you what to do — and what not to do — and are all based solidly upon the buy/sell signals generated by the Vital Sign indicators.

In the same way that a rocket is programmed to automatically "lock on" to its target — this system's approach to real estate timing can program you to automatically "lock on" to your target: the greatest real estate profits possible.

Cardinal Rule #1:
Invest with the Trend

The trend is your friend — don't fight it. *This is the most important rule of all.* When the trend is up, you can safely invest in real estate and make money. But when the trend is down, beware.

Your money is not safe, and you want to be out of the market until the trend turns up again.

When you use the Vital Sign indicators to invest with the trend, you are being a *selective* risk taker, not one who takes random risks. You will be using the same intelligent approach to real estate investing that Ted Williams used in hitting a baseball. The last player to hit .400 in the Major Leagues (.406 in 1941), he turned the art of hitting into a near science. His secret was simple: he trained himself to only swing at those pitches that were in certain areas of the strike zone, pitches that he knew he could hit for a high average. In other words, being *selective* was Ted Williams' ticket into the Hall of Fame.

While you can be great in baseball by only swinging at good pitches, you can be great in real estate by only participating in those trends that have the highest probability for making money . . . the market uptrends. This means that you should not place your primary emphasis on the traditional "location, location, location" theory of real estate success.

Never forget this: during rising markets, even poorly located properties go up in value. During falling markets, even the prices of well-located properties go down. In other words, as they say on the farm: "When the gun goes off, all the turkeys fly."

Cardinal Rule #2:
Be Comfortable Holding Cash

It is one of the great myths of real estate to say that if your money is not 100% invested, it is not "working" for you. This kind of thinking ignores the fact that *cash* is also an investment; an investment in the opportunity to buy real estate during times of doom and gloom, when cash is king and it is the asset everybody wants.

Some advisors tell you never to sell, to "buy and hold" real estate forever. *The Campbell Method* suggests another option: sell at market peaks and "buy and hold" U.S. Treasury Bills (which are government insured) until the market downtrend is over.

Cardinal Rule #3:
Forget the Past

A story is told about when Mark Twain once lost money on a business venture in 1880. A few years later, a good friend offered him another investment opportunity. Still upset about the previous loss, Twain declined the offer. This turned out to be a big mistake. Why? The friend was Alexander Graham Bell. The opportunity was a new invention called the *telephone.*

Let go of the past. The markets have no memory, only people do. The 1990's real estate crash in California depressed property values by 30-40%. By the end of each decade, prices were hitting new highs. Those individuals who believed market values would not recover missed a great buying opportunity.

Cardinal Rule #4:
Beware of the Crowd

All great investors are market contrarians. They buy panic and sell euphoria. This is because "the crowd" — driven by pure emotion rather than objectivity — tends to be *most wrong* during those critical times when it counts most to be right . . . namely at major market turning points.

Thus, the law of the pendulum can be applied to swings in the real estate prices: when mass public opinion reaches its maximum point of optimism or pessimism is precisely when the market is most likely to start moving in the opposite direction.

Let others follow the crowd. Analyze the market from your head– not your emotions — and follow the Vital Sign indicators instead.

Cardinal Rule #5:
Ride the Uptrend until the Trend Ends

Catching a market uptrend early and riding the trend to the very end, before you sell, guarantees the biggest real estate profits. While selling too soon may offer you smaller but more immediate profits — and give you immediate psychological gratification as a result of your success–this is clearly not the best way to maximize profits.

While it is true that you never go broke by taking a small profit, why limit yourself when prices are still trending higher? Go along for the ride, the whole ride, all the way to the end.

Cardinal Rule #6:
Be Patient Before You Buy or Sell.
Let the Market Do Its Work

Don't buy just because the price seems "low" and don't sell just because the price seems "high." In other words, don't try to guess how "low is low" or how "high is high." Instead, be patient and wait for the market to tell you for sure . . . when the trend changes.

Preconceived ideas about price levels have nothing to do with true profit potential. Market psychology (fear and greed) can drive prices to ridiculous levels of overvaluation and undervaluation. For this reason, avoid thinking in terms like: "The market is cheap, it can't go any lower" or "prices are too high, it's time to sell."

In waiting for the most profitable time to buy and sell real estate, you should use the same careful approach that you would use in looking for someone to marry: it pays to be alert, interested, and open-minded, but it does not pay to be in a hurry.

Cardinal Rule #7:
Be Self-Reliant. Don't be Influenced by the Media,
Financial Gurus, or Real Estate Agents

When you use the Vital Sign indicators to anticipate the direction of the market, you only need to rely on yourself to make intelligent buy/sell decisions. The decision to "call your own shots" is not based upon you being smarter than everyone else . . . but that the market is.

Regarding the media, never forget that its first order of business is to sell stories, not to accurately report factual information. Television, radio, and newspapers generally report on what the people want to hear. And whatever excites the public the most — whatever are the hottest trends in the market — the media often hypes them and talks about them like they will last forever.

Next, don't act on the *personal opinions* of financial gurus and experts. While these people are bright and articulate — and usually have impressive degrees from the best universities — history proves that their market forecasts are wrong as often as they are right.

Lastly, while real estate agents serve an important role in the real estate business, don't look to them for *objective* advice on real estate timing. For one thing, like all commissioned sales people, agents are biased. Unless they sell, they starve. Besides, the vast majority of real estate agents have little or no knowledge of identifying market cycles. So, when the market is overheated and near its peak, real estate agents — like the "crowd" in general — will advise you to hurry and "buy now" before prices rise further. Then, years later, when the market is tanking badly and probably near its market cycle bottom, these same agents are confident that you should "sell now" before prices drop even further.

To use real estate agents wisely, use them to carry out your market-timing strategy — not formulate it. You can also use your agent as a source of monthly data for Vital Sign indicator #1: *existing home sales*. As illustrated in Chapter 12, because demand is the key to real estate trends, tracking the trend for existing home sales will always give you an important clue about what's ahead for your local real estate market.

Be clear about this: no one cares about your money as much as you do. No matter what the media is reporting, or what the experts are saying, or what real estate agents want you to do, learn what you can from them — but become self-reliant in your decision-making.

Listen to market facts, not market opinions. Listen to the Vital Sign indicators.

Cardinal Rule #8:
Don't be Greedy

Fred Kelly, who wrote the investment book *Why You Win or Lose*, tells the following story that explains how greed and procrastination can hurt you.

A man has rigged up a turkey trap with a trail of corn leading into a big box with a hinged door. The man holds a long piece of twine, connected to the door, which he can use to pull the door shut when enough turkeys have wandered into the box.

There is a slight catch, however. Once the man shuts the door, he can't open it again. One day he had twelve turkeys in the box. Then one walked out, leaving eleven. "I should have pulled the string when there were twelve inside," he thought, "but maybe if I wait, he'll walk back in."

While the man was waiting for the twelfth turkey to return, two more turkeys walked out. "I should have been satisfied with eleven," he thought. "If just one more walks back in, I'll pull the string."

While he was waiting, three more turkeys walked out. Eventually, they all walked out and the man was left empty-handed.

The moral of this story is found in an old saying on Wall Street: "Bulls make money, bears make money, but pigs get slaughtered."

When it is time to sell, take what the market is willing to give you. Don't be greedy.

Cardinal Rule #9:
Hope is a Four-Letter Word

All successful investors will tell you that "hope" is a dirty word. Not only can hope keep you from selling at market peaks — because you hope prices will go higher — but hope can keep you from buying at market bottoms — because you hope prices will fall lower. Either way, when you hope, it costs you.

Whenever you hear a buyer or seller say "I hope" or "I wish," they are taking attention away from what they should be doing... identifying the trend of the market, and buying and selling accordingly.

The key to Cardinal Rule #9: *observe, adjust and prosper.*

Cardinal Rule #10:
Be Disciplined.
Know the Rules and Follow Them

Even when you know the rules, following them may be the most difficult rule of all. This is because emotions like hope, fear, greed, ego, and pride tend to be far more powerful than one's ability to exercise discipline and willpower to resist them.

Remember this: the real estate market rewards good habits and punishes bad habits. To change your habits to yield greater real estate rewards, just follow these *Ten Cardinal Rules* and you will be amazed at how only good things will happen.

The Difference between the Rich and Everyone Else: A Game Plan for Investing Money

"The rich are different from you and I," wrote F. Scott Fitzgerald. "Yes, they are," replied his friend Ernest Hemingway. "They have more money."

If you study wealthy people, you will find that there are other differences as well. For one, the rich know how to intelligently invest money. According to *The Millionaire Next Door* by Stanley and Danko: "There is a strong correlation between investment planning and wealth accumulation." In other words, the rich are careful to pursue the right investment opportunities that exist in the marketplace.

Because investments play a major role in building wealth, it is estimated that rich people get 70% of their income from investments and only 30% from wages.

For everyone else — the poor and the middle class — it is a completely different story. Statistics show that over 80% of their income comes from wages and less than 20% comes from investments. Furthermore, without a game plan for *correctly investing money*, Stanley and Danko's research shows that even if you make a good salary — with pay increases and fringe benefits — this is unlikely to make you rich.

So what is the best way for the average American to accumulate wealth or get rich? Investing in real estate may be your best choice. And why not? Ninety percent of all millionaires claim that investing in real estate is how they made a great deal of their money.

The Millionaire Next Door offers great encouragement to everyone who wants to get ahead in life. This book proves that by making the right investments, almost anyone with a steady job and a good investment game plan can get wealthy and achieve financial security. The best way to do this may be from investing in real estate. And when you take an intelligent, disciplined, and businesslike approach to real estate investing — in which you use *The Campbell Method* to buy when prices are cheap and to sell when they are expensive — you can be confident that you will be assisted up the success ladder at a much faster pace.

– Chapter 11 –

Putting It All Together: Trends Never End, They Only Change Direction

The winds and waves are always on the side of the ablest navigators.
— Edward Gibbon

Spotting the peaks and valleys of real estate cycles has always been the dream of both buyers and sellers. With the cyclical nature of the market, good times come, good times go, and then good times reappear again. The challenge for intelligent deci-sion-makers is to look for ways to profit from changing market trends, rather than just sitting back and — good or bad — passively accepting them.

Riding the market up is the way to make money grow; avoiding the ride down is the way to protect money from loss. This is the true wealth formula — and those who manage money according to its dictates will be far wealthier than those who do not.

It stands to reason that those who respond — and adjust — to changing real estate trends will achieve higher returns than those who do not. If you are a prospective homebuyer or a real estate investor, *why not buy* at a market cycle bottom when prices are depressed? And if you already own real estate, *why not sell* when prices are high at a market cycle peak?

Your Home is Your Piggy-Bank

Even though the profit motive is ever-present in the American culture, a home will always mean different things to different people. Most often, it is far more than a pure investment asset like stocks, bonds, or owning a home to rent out. By some estimates, however, 75% of an American's net worth is in their homes. For most of you — like it or not — this means that your financial futures are hitched to real estate. Major swings in the real estate market, therefore, are likely to have a major impact on your present and future economic well-being.

So how do you become more successful in real estate? You do this by making good decisions. And how do you make good decisions? By buying and selling according to the major trends. And how do you identify major trends? By following the Vital Sign indicators.

The Campbell Method gives you a game plan for maximizing real estate profits. You won't suffer the confusion that besets most real estate buyers and sellers. When you follow the Vital Sign indicators — and adhere to the Three Market Truths and the Ten Cardinal Rules — *The Campbell Method* automatically programs you to know when real estate should be bought and sold.

And while you can't always expect to hit the market peaks and valleys right on the nose every time, you can expect to know when the winds of market change are coming your way — and what to do in response. The challenge is great, but so are the rewards. We have all heard the expression, *"When all else fails, read the directions."* And so it is with making good real estate decisions: *"When in doubt, follow what the market is telling you to do."*

Using Vital Sign Charts

In a free-market economy, the laws of supply and demand will always determine the direction of real estate prices and the best way for you to accurately measure supply and demand in the real estate market is with the Vital Sign charts. With the use of market momentum calculations, these charts compare the recent past with what is happening today. This allows you to measure the underlying strength (or weakness) of the market, telling you whether the future favors higher or lower property values.

With minimal expertise on how to read a Vital Sign chart, an individual is given the forward vision to stay ahead of trends. Only rarely will you find yourself saying: "I'm not sure what the market is telling me to do." When this happens, just check the Vital Sign charts every month and the answer will likely be there.

To make the charting process even more valuable, it helps to commit your plan of action to writing. For example — in determining when to sell — you might pre-establish your decision points like this: "When the momentum line for existing home sales and new home building permits fall below the "0" line, I'll look at interest rates. If interest rates are rising, I'll sell immediately. If interest rates are falling, I'll wait until mortgage loan defaults start to rise before I sell."

This simple exercise will help you to focus on market facts — and help you to forget about hope and wishful thinking — for intelligent decision-making.

Of course, the *more* that the Vital Signs show market strength or market weakness, the *more* they confirm the direction in which prices are likely to move. The bottom line, however, is this: rising demand is the pillar of the real estate market. Thus, even though acting on multiple Vital Sign signals is always recommended, there is a fast and accurate way to measure whether "demand" is increasing or decreasing in your specific city.

**The K.I.S.S. Method
("Keep It Simple, Sweetheart")
For Tracking Trends**

A Senate committee once questioned J.P. Morgan, the most powerful financier of his day, about why the stock market crashed. "Too many sellers," he answered. While Morgan was being somewhat flippant, his reply could not have been more accurate. This is due to the fact that changes in market conditions — and all market trends — can be explained by *imbalances* between the number of buyers and sellers.

Applying this same economic logic to anticipating real estate trends, the K.I.S.S. method requires that you only follow Vital Sign #1: *existing home sales*, and Vital Sign #2, *new home building permits*. Therefore, to get a fast yet insightful "read" on your local market, these two indicators are excellent to follow for these reasons:

First, you can count on home sale and new home building activity to be accurate leading indicators to price movement. This relationship is illustrated in Chapters 7 and 8.

Second, the monthly market data for these two Vital Sign indicators is relatively easy to obtain. A good source of home sale activity is real estate agents, who can provide you with both historic and current monthly home sales data for the Multiple Listing Service (MLS). A good source of building permit activity is available online from the U.S. Census Bureau at www.census.gov/const/www/permitsindex.html.

Will real estate agents provide you with this historic home sale data . . . and provide you with the most current monthly updates? Most likely, the answer is "yes." Because real estate is a highly competitive business, where agents spend much of their time prospecting for new buyers and sellers, most agents will probably jump at the opportunity to be of assistance.

(Note: If you want to purchase a computer program that will *automatically — and instantly —* do the "market momentum" Vital

Sign calculations and Vital Sign charts shown in this book, see page 191 for ordering instructions.)

How to React to Market Fluctuations

You open the newspaper and read the following headline: "Real Estate Market in Tailspin -Prices Tumble." How do you react? Most people are only elated when property values are climbing higher. Then, after prices start to sink, they are looking for anti-depressants. We were all taught that rising real estate markets are good and falling markets are bad — but this is not *always* true.

If you are a prospective homebuyer, or if you are looking to invest in rental property, do you prefer lower or higher real estate prices? Obviously, this question answers itself. Therefore, if you are a prospective buyer, "gloomy" real estate headlines should put a smile on your face.

In real estate, you can turn adversity into opportunity. The key is to not judge markets or trends — as good or bad, but to be ready for them and take advantage of them. As they say in golf: "Every shot makes *someone* happy."

Warning! Market Knowledge without Action Pays No Dividends

Having superior information is not enough to profit in real estate. You must also be capable of adjusting to changing market conditions. Thus, when the Vital Sign indicators are giving you signals to buy or sell, don't act like a deer caught in the headlights and freeze and do nothing.

The meek may or may not inherit the earth, but it is almost guaranteed that they *won't* make the *most* money in real estate. Timing — and assertiveness — pay the biggest dividends in the long-term. Remember the Noah Principle: *Predicting rain doesn't count, building arks does.*

Betting on the Right Trends

Investing in real estate is a lot like horse racing. Who is most likely to win the race? Is it the jockey that is the smartest, most self-confident, or highly motivated? No, nine times out of ten, the jockey who wins the race is the one riding the best horse.

This same principle applies to real estate investing. The investors who are the most successful are those who ride the best trends.

In a horse race, the horses are handicapped. The better the horse, the better the odds. This means that the two to one *favorite* is ten times more likely to win the race than the 20 to one *long shot*. From a purely mathematical standpoint, on which horse would you place your money — the favorite or the long shot?

But what if the jockey riding the long shot tries harder by applying the whip more? Will this increase his chances of winning? Not really, because the jockey on the best horse can do the same to his horse.

This means that if you are riding the wrong horse, hard work isn't likely to make you successful at the racetrack or in real estate. Riding a market downtrend in real estate is the same as riding the wrong horse at the racetrack. It is no different than betting on a 20 to one long shot.

Does this suggest that successful people aren't smart or that they don't work hard? Not at all. But it does say that these virtues are not always positively correlated with success.

Today, more and more Americans are coming to the realization that in this land of great opportunity, it is becoming more and more difficult to get ahead. So if you are looking for financial security, it is wise to look to real estate. By working hard, having superior knowledge, and riding the right trends, you can achieve enormous success. And while it is nice to do all three, when you know how to ride the right trends, hard work and superior knowledge are optional.

The Campbell Method:
Profit by Design — Not by Accident

Just because the experts, the economists, and the media can't see it coming, this doesn't mean that you have to be caught by surprise by major turning points in the market. And you don't have to try to second-guess population trends or what the Federal Reserve Board is going to do to the economy next. From now on — to predict future trends–get your hands on some Vital Sign charts and see what they are saying.

Real estate trends do not change by accident or out of the clear blue. The market signs are always there for you to see. Now you know where to look. And by doing momentum calculations on these Vital Sign indicators, you are actually applying Newton's law of physics to the market — that a trend in motion will stay in motion until something causes it to reverse.

Is it time to buy or bail out? While the general public is looking backwards — and expecting the prevailing trend to continue indefinitely — you will be *looking forward* for signs of change. This allows you to "act early" instead of "react late" when it is time to enter and exit the market.

Admittedly, breaking away from the crowd, being a contrary thinker, and having the discipline to follow a set of proven rules (instead of your emotions) is never easy. However, when your money is on the line, never be complacent. Sure, real estate will most likely continue to be a good long-term investment, but anything can happen at any time. The next major turn in the real estate market may be years away . . . or months away. While no one has a crystal ball, the market itself *will* tell you what it is going to do next.

For whatever reason that you own real estate — whether it is a home to live in or for rental income and capital appreciation — remember this: ignoring the trend of the market will always result in a lower return-on-investment than could be achieved otherwise.

With that understanding, this book shall end as it began.

When it comes to making money in real estate, nothing beats good timing.

– Chapter 12 –

Final Words: A Real Estate Timing Breakthrough

*Timing and strategy are the redwoods of real estate success.
Everything else is a bonsai.*
— Robert M. Campbell

Roger Bannister broke the four-minute mile in 1954. Before he did it, everyone "knew" it could not be done. Once the feat was accomplished, however, a lot of runners quickly broke the four-minute barrier as well.

Psychologists tell us that, in life, we tend to become what we expect to become. In an odd sort of way, our lives ultimately turn out to be some sort of self-fulfilling prophecy. We become our vision. You see this happen over and over again: a person ignores the doubters and naysayers, pursues his dream, and accomplishes the impossible.

Roger Bannister's breakthrough created a new vision of what was possible for long-distance runners. This led to faster and faster performances.

It is my wish that *The Campbell Method* — and the real estate timing breakthrough revealed in this book — create a new vision and dream for you.

It will inspire you to buy and sell the home that you live in more profitably.

It will give you the confidence to buy your first rental property — to buy it during a market cycle bottom when prices are low and then sell it years later for a spectacular profit when prices are peaking.

Or maybe it will motivate you to get really filthy rich in real estate.

Whatever your dream, whatever your own personal vision, remember this: get started, pursue it with vigor, make the most of every advantage you can give yourself, and know that nothing is impossible. Just ask Roger Bannister.

Yours truly,

Appendix

Stock Market Timing and Recession

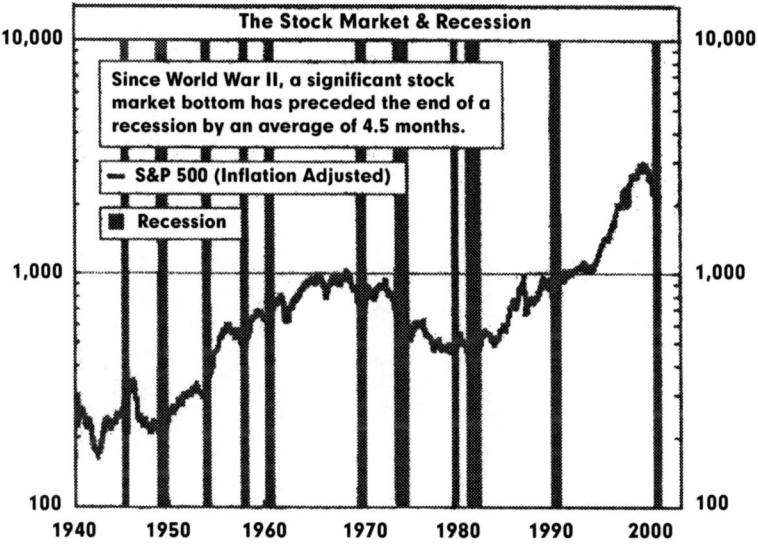

Source—Pinnacle Data

Economic recessions have historically presented stock market investors with excellent opportunities to buy stocks. The chart above is evidence of this, showing that since the end of World War II, significant stock market bottoms were made during most U.S. recessions. On average, these stock market bottoms occurred about three to seven months before the recession ended, proving that acting according to the laws of contrary thinking can be highly profitable.

This same contrarian principle applies to downturns in real estate cycles, where the best opportunities to buy occur when homes and investment properties are "on sale" and not simply "for sale."

Market Momentum Worksheet
Vital Sign #1
Existing Home Sales (San Diego, CA): 1988-2006

Column A Month	Column B Month and Year	Column C Vital Sign Monthly Data	Column D 12-month Exponential Moving Average	Column E Vital Sign Momentum Reading
1	Jan-1988	2216	2216	
2	Feb-1988	2329	2233	
3	Mar-1988	3182	2379	
4	Apr-1988	3671	2578	
5	May-1988	3884	2779	
6	Jun-1988	5164	3146	
7	Jul-1988	4613	3371	
8	Aug-1988	4814	3593	
9	Sept-1988	5003	3810	
10	Oct-1988	4185	3868	
11	Nov-1988	4223	3922	
12	Dec-1988	4651	4034	
13	Jan-1989	3320	3925	77
14	Feb-1989	3037	3788	70
15	Mar-1989	4629	3917	65
16	Apr-1989	4306	3977	54
17	May-1989	4417	4045	46
18	Jun-1989	4900	4176	33
19	Jul-1989	4063	4159	23
20	Aug-1989	4871	4268	19
21	Sept-1989	4336	4279	12
22	Oct-1989	4376	4294	11
23	Nov-1989	3735	4208	7
24	Dec-1989	3795	4144	3
25	Jan-1990	3037	3974	1
26	Feb-1990	2752	3786	0
27	Mar-1990	3901	3804	-3
28	Apr-1990	3414	3744	-6
29	May-1990	3626	3726	-8

30	Jun-1990	3605	3707	-11
31	Jul-1990	3319	3647	-12
32	Aug-1990	3796	3670	-14
33	Sept-1990	2637	3511	-18
34	Oct-1990	2734	3392	-21
35	Nov-1990	2223	3212	-24
36	Dec-1990	2117	3044	-27
37	Jan-1991	1476	2802	-29
38	Feb-1991	1448	2594	-31
39	Mar-1991	1952	2495	-34
40	Apr-1991	2277	2461	-34
41	May-1991	2854	2522	-32
42	Jun-1991	2629	2539	-32
43	Jul-1991	2767	2574	-29
44	Aug-1991	2553	2571	-30
45	Sept-1991	1963	2478	-29
46	Oct-1991	1993	2403	-29
47	Nov-1991	1813	2311	-28
48	Dec-1991	1951	2256	-26
49	Jan-1992	1548	2147	-23
50	Feb-1992	1475	2044	-21
51	Mar-1992	2268	2078	-17
52	Apr-1992	2521	2147	-13
53	May-1992	2290	2169	-14
54	Jun-1992	2309	2190	-14
55	Jul-1992	2330	2212	-14
56	Aug-1992	1897	2163	-16
57	Sept-1992	1879	2120	-14
58	Oct-1992	2356	2156	-10
59	Nov-1992	2150	2155	-7
60	Dec-1992	2757	2248	0
61	Jan-1993	1703	2164	1
62	Feb-1993	1751	2100	3
63	Mar-1993	2262	2125	2
64	Apr-1993	2461	2177	1
65	May-1993	2365	2206	2
66	Jun-1993	2630	2271	4
67	Jul-1993	2690	2335	6

68	Aug-1993	2604	2377	10
69	Sept-1993	2621	2414	14
70	Oct-1993	2276	2393	11
71	Nov-1993	2261	2373	10
72	Dec-1993	2717	2426	8
73	Jan-1994	1936	2350	9
74	Feb-1994	1795	2265	8
75	Mar-1994	2815	2350	11
76	Apr-1994	2695	2403	10
77	May-1994	2751	2456	11
78	Jun-1994	2808	2510	11
79	Jul-1994	2369	2489	7
80	Aug-1994	2451	2483	4
81	Sept-1994	2282	2452	2
82	Oct-1994	1891	2366	-1
83	Nov-1994	1901	2294	-3
84	Dec-1994	1996	2248	-7
85	Jan-1995	1330	2107	-10
86	Feb-1995	1280	1980	-13
87	Mar-1995	2016	1985	-15
88	Apr-1995	1734	1947	-19
89	May-1995	2053	1963	-20
90	Jun-1995	2322	2018	-20
91	Jul-1995	1889	1998	-20
92	Aug-1995	2607	2092	-16
93	Sept-1995	2136	2099	-14
94	Oct-1995	2082	2096	-11
95	Nov-1995	1960	2075	-10
96	Dec-1995	2127	2083	-7
97	Jan-1996	1662	2018	-4
98	Feb-1996	1750	1977	0
99	Mar-1996	2426	2046	3
100	Apr-1996	2623	2135	10
101	May-1996	2835	2243	14
102	Jun-1996	2579	2294	14
103	Jul-1996	2690	2355	18
104	Aug-1996	2691	2407	15
105	Sept-1996	2205	2376	13

106	Oct-1996	2292	2363	13
107	Nov-1996	2026	2311	11
108	Dec-1996	2236	2299	10
109	Jan-1997	1890	2237	11
110	Feb-1997	1947	2192	11
111	Mar-1997	2443	2231	9
112	Apr-1997	2757	2312	8
113	May-1997	2926	2406	7
114	Jun-1997	2905	2483	8
115	Jul-1997	3121	2581	10
116	Aug-1997	3146	2668	11
117	Sept-1997	2924	2707	14
118	Oct-1997	3117	2770	17
119	Nov-1997	2383	2711	17
120	Dec-1997	2887	2738	19
121	Jan-1998	2076	2636	18
122	Feb-1998	2308	2586	18
123	Mar-1998	3313	2867	21
124	Apr-1998	3803	2867	24
125	May-1998	3795	3010	25
126	Jun-1998	4384	3413	30
127	Jul-1998	4468	3413	32
128	Aug-1998	3647	3449	29
129	Sept-1998	3579	3469	24
130	Oct-1998	3335	3448	28
131	Nov-1998	2731	3338	23
132	Dec-1998	3221	3320	21
133	Jan-1999	2465	3189	21
134	Feb-1999	2848	3136	21
135	Mar-1999	4111	3286	22
136	Apr-1999	4055	3404	19
137	May-1999	3927	3485	16
138	Jun-1999	4582	3654	13
139	Jul-1999	4308	3754	10
140	Aug-1999	4178	3819	11
141	Sept-1999	3750	3809	10
142	Oct-1999	3374	3742	9
143	Nov-1999	3131	3648	9

144	Dec-1999	3274	3590	8
145	Jan-2000	2475	3419	7
146	Feb-2000	2885	3337	6
147	Mar-2000	4146	3461	5
148	Apr-2000	3661	3492	3
149	May-2000	3982	3567	2
150	Jun-2000	4304	3681	1
151	Jul-2000	3541	3659	-3
152	Aug-2000	4023	3715	-3
153	Sept-2000	3866	3738	-2
154	Oct-2000	3627	3721	-1
155	Nov-2000	3238	3647	0
156	Dec-2000	3119	3566	-1
157	Jan-2001	2456	3395	-1
158	Feb-2001	2396	3241	-3
159	Mar-2001	3581	3294	-5
160	Apr-2001	3341	3301	-5
161	May-2001	3647	3354	-6
162	Jun-2001	4061	3463	-6
163	Jul-2001	3905	3531	-4
164	Aug-2001	4126	3622	-2
165	Sept-2001	3092	3541	-5
166	Oct-2001	3082	3470	-7
167	Nov-2001	2600	3336	-9
168	Dec-2001	2839	3260	-9
169	Jan-2002	2744	3181	-6
170	Feb-2002	2998	3152	-3
171	Mar-2002	3951	3275	-1
172	Apr-2002	4012	3537	3
173	May-2002	4353	3537	5
174	Jun-2002	3964	3603	7
175	Jul-2002	4050	3671	6
176	Aug-2002	4035	3727	3
177	Sept-2002	3279	3658	3
178	Oct-2002	3662	3659	5
179	Nov-2002	2897	3542	6
180	Dec-2002	3667	3561	9
181	Jan-2003	2888	3458	9

182	Feb-2003	2866	3367	7
183	Mar-2003	3453	3480	3
184	Apr-2003	4171	3502	3
185	May-2003	4132	3598	2
186	Jun-2003	4028	3665	2
187	Jul-2003	4715	3826	4
188	Aug-2003	4860	3985	7
189	Sept-2003	4416	4051	11
190	Oct-2003	4081	4071	11
191	Nov-2003	3508	3985	13
192	Dec-2003	4013	3989	12
193	Jan-2004	2958	3830	11
194	Feb-2004	3267	3743	11
195	Mar-2004	4283	3827	13
196	Apr-2004	5047	4014	15
197	May-2004	4417	4076	13
198	Jun-2004	4991	4217	15
199	Jul-2004	4543	4267	12
200	Aug-2004	4246	4264	7
201	Sep-2004	3775	4189	3
202	Oct-2004	3446	4074	0
203	Nov-2004	3247	3947	-1
204	Dec-2004	3433	3868	-3
205	Jan-2005	2490	3656	-5
206	Feb-2005	2500	3478	-7
207	Mar-2005	3729	3517	-8
208	Apr-2005	4095	3606	-10
209	May-2005	4420	3731	-8
210	June-2005	4441	3840	-9
211	Jul-2005	4028	3869	-9
212	Aug-2005	3937	3880	-9
213	Sep-2005	3499	3821	-9
214	Oct-2005	3155	3719	-9
215	Nov-2005	2751	3570	-10
216	Dec-2005	2747	3443	-11
217	Jan-2006	2093	3236	-12
218	Feb-2006	2163	3070	-12
219	Mar-2006	3014	3062	-13

220	Apr-2006	2882	3034	-16
221	May-2006	3055	3037	-19
222	Jun-2006	3114	3054	-20
223	Jul-2006	2531	2973	-23
224	Aug-2006	2767	2942	-24
225	Sept-2006	2322	2846	-26
226	Oct-2006	2336	2768	-26
227				
228				
229				
230				
231				
232				
233				
234				
235				
236				
237				
238				
239				
240				
241				
242				
243				
244				
245				
246				
247				
248				
249				
250				
251				
252				

Source: DataQuick Information Systems

Note: To chart Vital Sign #1, a 12-month exponential moving average (EMA) was used instead of the standard 12-month moving average explained in Chapter 6. The smoothing constant for a

12-month EMA is .1538. Here is the formula used in the above calculations:

Last month's EMA + ((Data for current month − Last month's EMA) x .1538)

Market Momentum Worksheet
Vital Sign #2
New Home Building Permits (San Diego): 1988-2006

Column A Month	Column B Month and Year	Column C Vital Sign Monthly Data	Column D 12-month Exponential Moving Average	Column E Vital Sign Momentum Reading
1	Jan-1988	995	195	
2	Feb-1988	1162	1021	
3	Mar-1988	2751	1287	
4	Apr-1988	2689	1502	
5	May-1988	2009	1580	
6	Jun-1988	2540	1728	
7	Jul-1988	1727	1728	
8	Aug-1988	3465	1995	
9	Sept-1988	2516	2075	
10	Oct-1988	4180	2399	
11	Nov-1988	3728	2603	
12	Dec-1988	792	2324	
13	Jan-1989	1404	2183	119
14	Feb-1989	1432	2067	103
15	Mar-1989	1781	2023	57
16	Apr-1989	1321	1915	27
17	May-1989	1806	1899	20
18	Jun-1989	1481	1834	6
19	Jul-1989	1985	1857	8
20	Aug-1989	1302	1772	-11
21	Sept-1989	675	1603	-23
22	Oct-1989	1281	1554	-35
23	Nov-1989	2037	1628	-37
24	Dec-1989	2205	1717	-26
25	Jan-1990	3102	1930	-12
26	Feb-1990	1692	1893	-8
27	Mar-1990	1579	1845	-9
28	Apr-1990	1315	1763	-8
29	May-1990	1222	1680	-12

30	Jun-1990	1373	1633	-11
31	Jul-1990	860	1514	-18
32	Aug-1990	1361	1491	-16
33	Sept-1990	736	1374	-14
34	Oct-1990	987	1315	-15
35	Nov-1990	696	1220	-25
36	Dec-1990	873	1166	-32
37	Jan-1991	474	1060	-45
38	Feb-1991	654	997	-47
39	Mar-1991	2729	1264	-32
40	Apr-1991	704	1178	-33
41	May-1991	282	1040	-38
42	Jun-1991	708	989	-39
43	Jul-1991	507	915	-40
44	Aug-1991	509	852	-43
45	Sept-1991	299	767	-44
46	Oct-1991	430	715	-46
47	Nov-1991	292	650	-47
48	Dec-1991	320	599	-49
49	Jan-1992	843	637	-40
50	Feb-1992	768	657	-34
51	Mar-1992	719	667	-47
52	Apr-1992	489	639	-46
53	May-1992	554	626	-40
54	Jun-1992	759	647	-35
55	Jul-1992	479	621	-32
56	Aug-1992	346	579	-32
57	Sept-1992	393	550	-28
58	Oct-1992	218	499	-30
59	Nov-1992	163	447	-31
60	Dec-1992	328	429	-28
61	Jan-1993	414	427	-33
62	Feb-1993	290	406	-38
63	Mar-1993	476	416	-38
64	Apr-1993	488	427	-33
65	May-1993	448	431	-31
66	Jun-1993	620	460	-29
67	Jul-1993	754	505	-19

68	Aug-1993	310	475	-18
69	Sept-1993	347	455	-17
70	Oct-1993	526	466	-7
71	Nov-1993	486	469	5
72	Dec-1993	443	465	8
73	Jan-1994	498	470	10
74	Feb-1994	478	471	16
75	Mar-1994	571	487	17
76	Apr-1994	586	502	17
77	May-1994	779	545	26
78	Jun-1994	804	585	27
79	Jul-1994	320	544	8
80	Aug-1994	642	559	18
81	Sept-1994	616	568	25
82	Oct-1994	640	579	24
83	Nov-1994	387	549	17
84	Dec-1994	614	559	20
85	Jan-1995	452	543	15
86	Feb-1995	330	510	8
87	Mar-1995	375	489	1
88	Apr-1995	826	541	8
89	May-1995	846	588	8
90	Jun-1995	649	597	2
91	Jul-1995	426	571	5
92	Aug-1995	688	589	5
93	Sept-1995	643	597	5
94	Oct-1995	456	576	-1
95	Nov-1995	493	563	2
96	Dec-1995	424	542	-3
97	Jan-1996	352	512	-6
98	Feb-1996	501	511	0
99	Mar-1996	667	535	9
100	Apr-1996	667	555	3
101	May-1996	605	563	-4
102	Jun-1996	523	557	-7
103	Jul-1996	912	611	7
104	Aug-1996	447	586	-1
105	Sept-1996	467	568	-5

106	Oct-1996	676	584	2
107	Nov-1996	528	576	2
108	Dec-1996	523	568	5
109	Jan-1997	591	571	11
110	Feb-1997	675	587	15
111	Mar-1997	590	588	10
112	Apr-1997	829	625	13
113	May-1997	828	656	17
114	Jun-1997	1157	733	32
115	Jul-1997	938	765	25
116	Aug-1997	981	798	36
117	Sept-1997	1139	850	50
118	Oct-1997	1961	1021	75
119	Nov-1997	845	994	73
120	Dec-1997	773	960	69
121	Jan-1998	718	923	62
122	Feb-1998	994	934	59
123	Mar-1998	882	926	58
124	Apr-1998	941	928	49
125	May-1998	1019	942	44
126	Jun-1998	1503	1028	40
127	Jul-1998	1083	1037	36
128	Aug-1998	1822	1158	45
129	Sept-1998	766	1097	29
130	Oct-1998	980	1079	6
131	Nov-1998	755	1029	4
132	Dec-1998	676	975	2
133	Jan-1999	1878	1114	21
134	Feb-1999	821	1069	14
135	Mar-1999	1679	1163	26
136	Apr-1999	1871	1272	37
137	May-1999	1497	1306	39
138	Jun-1999	1583	1349	31
139	Jul-1999	1252	1334	29
140	Aug-1999	1272	1324	14
141	Sept-1999	1817	1400	28
142	Oct-1999	910	1325	23
143	Nov-1999	723	1232	20

144	Dec-1999	1124	1216	25
145	Jan-2000	1183	1211	9
146	Feb-2000	967	1173	10
147	Mar-2000	1965	1295	11
148	Apr-2000	1501	1327	4
149	May-2000	1178	1304	0
150	Jun-2000	2445	1479	10
151	Jul-2000	911	1392	4
152	Aug-2000	1241	1369	3
153	Sept-2000	956	1305	-7
154	Oct-2000	1083	1271	-4
155	Nov-2000	981	1226	0
156	Dec-2000	1516	1271	5
157	Jan-2001	1881	1365	13
158	Feb-2001	1187	1337	14
159	Mar-2001	937	1276	-1
160	Apr-2001	1373	1291	-3
161	May-2001	1545	1330	2
162	Jun-2001	1755	1395	-6
163	Jul-2001	1175	1361	-2
164	Aug-2001	1152	1329	-3
165	Sept-2001	1151	1302	0
166	Oct-2001	1575	1344	6
167	Nov-2001	849	1268	3
168	Dec-2001	1070	1237	-3
169	Jan-2002	1835	1329	-3
170	Feb-2002	1008	1280	-4
171	Mar-2002	1402	1299	2
172	Apr-2002	1542	1336	4
173	May-2002	1184	1313	1
174	Jun-2002	1235	1301	-7
175	Jul-2002	1075	1266	-7
176	Aug-2002	1724	1336	1
177	Sept-2002	1157	1309	1
178	Oct-2002	1194	1291	-4
179	Nov-2002	1432	1313	-4
180	Dec-2002	950	1257	2
181	Jan-2003	1167	1243	-6

182	Feb-2003	2215	1393	9
183	Mar-2003	2426	1552	19
184	Apr-2003	1527	1548	16
185	May-2003	1287	1508	15
186	Jun-2003	1089	1443	11
187	Jul-2003	1300	1421	12
188	Aug-2003	1281	1400	5
189	Sept-2003	1759	1455	11
190	Oct-2003	1425	1450	12
191	Nov-2003	1151	1404	7
192	Dec-2003	1687	1448	15
193	Jan-2004	1289	1423	14
194	Feb-2004	1479	1432	3
195	Mar-2004	1664	1468	-5
196	Apr-2004	1918	1537	-1
197	May-2004	1456	1524	1
198	Jun-2004	1492	1519	5
199	Jul-2004	1103	1455	2
200	Aug-2004	1658	1487	6
201	Sep-2004	1335	1463	1
202	Oct-2004	927	1381	-5
203	Nov-2004	1553	1407	0
204	Dec-2004	1432	1411	-3
205	Jan-2005	1461	1419	0
206	Feb-2005	921	1342	-6
207	Mar-2005	2436	1510	3
208	Apr-2005	1270	1473	-4
209	May-2005	1824	1527	0
210	Jun-2005	1196	2476	-3
211	Jul-2005	1355	1458	0
212	Aug-2005	1437	1455	-2
213	Sep-2005	1249	1423	-3
214	Oct-2005	633	1301	-6
215	Nov-2005	801	1244	-13
216	Dec-2005	674	1140	-19
217	Jan-2006	627	1061	-25
218	Feb-2006	1180	1079	-20
219	Mar-2006	1122	1086	-28

220	Apr-2006	701	1027	-30
221	May-2006	937	1013	-34
222	Jun-2006	1985	1162	-21
223	Jul-2006	1252	1176	-19
224	Aug-2006	557	1081	-26
225	Sept-2006	591	1006	-29
226	Oct-2006	831	979	-25
227				
228				
229				
230				
231				
232				
233				
234				
235				
236				
237				
238				
239				
240				
241				
242				
243				
244				
245				
246				
247				
248				
249				
250				
251				
252				

Source: DataQuick Information Systems

Note: To chart Vital Sign #2, a 12-month exponential moving average (EMA) was used instead of the standard 12-month moving average explained in Chapter 6. The smoothing constant for a

12-month EMA is .1538. Here is the formula used in the above calculations:

**Current EMA = Last month's EMA +
((Data for current month − Last month's EMA) x .1538)**

Market Momentum Worksheet
Vital Sign #3
Notices of Default (San Diego, CA): 1982-2006

Column A Month	Column B Month and Year	Column C Vital Sign Monthly Data	Column D 12-month Moving Average	Column E Vital Sign Momentum Reading
1	Jan-1982	1293		
2	Feb-1982	1340		
3	Mar-1982	1440		
4	Apr-1982	1484		
5	May-1982	1238		
6	Jun-1982	1398		
7	Jul-1982	1317		
8	Aug-1982	1412		
9	Sept-1982	1180		
10	Oct-1982	1280		
11	Nov-1982	1259		
12	Dec-1982	1280	1327	
13	Jan-1983	1340	1331	
14	Feb-1983	1234	1322	
15	Mar-1983	1438	1322	
16	Apr-1983	1317	1307	
17	May-1983	1145	1300	
18	Jun-1983	1059	1272	
18	Jul-1983	1038	1249	
20	Aug-1983	1063	1219	
21	Sept-1983	960	1201	
22	Oct-1983	982	1176	
23	Nov-1983	973	1152	
24	Dec-1983	973	1127	-15
25	Jan-1984	982	1097	-18
26	Feb-1984	859	1066	-19
27	Mar-1984	1015	1031	-22
28	Apr-1984	853	992	-24

29	May-1984	1198	996	-23
30	Jun-1984	775	973	-24
31	Jul-1984	922	963	-23
32	Aug-1984	982	956	-22
33	Sept-1984	690	934	-22
34	Oct-1984	1029	938	-20
35	Nov-1984	731	917	-20
36	Dec-1984	628	889	-21
37	Jan-1985	845	877	-20
38	Feb-1985	720	866	-19
39	Mar-1985	854	852	-17
40	Apr-1985	813	849	-14
41	May-1985	775	814	-18
42	Jun-1985	711	808	-17
43	Jul-1985	761	795	-17
44	Aug-1985	827	782	-18
45	Sept-1985	836	794	-15
46	Oct-1985	771	773	-18
47	Nov-1985	647	766	-17
48	Dec-1985	805	780	-12
49	Jan-1986	739	772	-12
50	Feb-1986	654	766	-12
51	Mar-1986	804	762	-11
52	Apr-1986	854	765	-10
53	May-1986	754	764	-6
54	Jun-1986	727	765	-5
55	Jul-1986	674	758	-5
56	Aug-1986	670	745	-5
57	Sept-1986	717	735	-7
58	Oct-1986	725	730	-5
59	Nov-1986	601	727	-5
60	Dec-1986	732	721	-8
61	Jan-1987	731	720	-7
62	Feb-1987	552	712	-7
63	Mar-1987	720	705	-8
64	Apr-1987	691	691	-10
65	May-1987	620	680	-11
66	Jun-1987	691	677	-11

67	Jul-1987	628	673	-11
68	Aug-1987	637	670	-10
69	Sept-1987	608	661	-10
70	Oct-1987	635	654	-11
71	Nov-1987	559	650	-11
72	Dec-1987	603	640	-11
73	Jan-1988	612	630	-13
74	Feb-1988	584	632	-11
75	Mar-1988	713	632	-10
76	Apr-1988	592	624	-10
77	May-1988	609	623	-8
78	Jun-1988	623	617	-9
79	Jul-1988	518	608	-10
80	Aug-1988	602	605	-10
81	Sept-1988	543	599	-9
82	Oct-1988	536	591	-10
83	Nov-1988	474	584	-10
84	Dec-1988	545	579	-9
85	Jan-1989	570	576	-9
86	Feb-1989	516	570	-10
87	Mar-1989	588	560	-11
88	Apr-1989	507	553	-11
89	May-1989	604	552	-11
90	Jun-1989	661	555	-10
91	Jul-1989	483	552	-9
92	Aug-1989	627	555	-8
93	Sept-1989	559	556	-7
94	Oct-1989	585	560	-5
95	Nov-1989	539	565	-3
96	Dec-1989	503	562	-3
97	Jan-1990	585	563	-2
98	Feb-1990	562	567	-1
99	Mar-1990	666	573	2
100	Apr-1990	645	585	6
101	May-1990	748	597	8
102	Jun-1990	556	588	6
103	Jul-1990	718	608	10
104	Aug-1990	694	613	11

105	Sept-1990	650	621	12
106	Oct-1990	762	636	14
107	Nov-1990	713	650	15
108	Dec-1990	706	667	19
109	Jan-1991	789	684	21
110	Feb-1991	762	701	24
111	Mar-1991	889	719	25
112	Apr-1991	888	740	26
113	May-1991	956	757	27
114	Jun-1991	929	788	34
115	Jul-1991	922	805	32
116	Aug-1991	1094	838	37
117	Sept-1991	849	855	38
118	Oct-1991	1004	875	38
119	Nov-1991	838	886	36
120	Dec-1991	1007	911	37
121	Jan-1992	1052	933	36
122	Feb-1992	916	945	35
123	Mar-1992	1120	965	34
124	Apr-1992	1063	979	32
125	May-1992	861	971	28
126	Jun-1992	1010	978	24
127	Jul-1992	1101	993	23
128	Aug-1992	1011	986	18
129	Sept-1992	1065	1004	17
130	Oct-1992	915	997	14
131	Nov-1992	869	999	13
132	Dec-1992	1074	1005	10
133	Jan-1993	1108	1009	8
134	Feb-1993	1010	1017	8
135	Mar-1993	1313	1033	7
136	Apr-1993	1089	1036	6
137	May-1993	945	1043	7
138	Jun-1993	1119	1052	8
139	Jul-1993	1051	1047	5
140	Aug-1993	1019	1048	6
141	Sept-1993	1009	1043	4
142	Oct-1993	931	1045	5

143	Nov-1993	960	1052	5
144	Dec-1993	967	1043	4
145	Jan-1994	903	1026	2
146	Feb-1994	820	1011	-1
147	Mar-1994	1124	995	-4
148	Apr-1994	940	982	-5
149	May-1994	904	979	-6
150	Jun-1994	924	963	-8
151	Jul-1994	818	943	-10
152	Aug-1994	927	936	-11
153	Sept-1994	931	929	-11
154	Oct-1994	822	920	-12
155	Nov-1994	767	904	-14
156	Dec-1994	874	896	-14
157	Jan-1995	886	895	-13
158	Feb-1995	846	897	-11
159	Mar-1995	1077	893	-10
160	Apr-1995	873	887	-10
161	May-1995	963	892	-9
162	Jun-1995	964	896	-7
163	Jul-1995	875	900	-5
164	Aug-1995	1025	909	-3
165	Sept-1995	843	901	-3
166	Oct-1995	970	914	-1
167	Nov-1995	1038	936	4
168	Dec-1995	891	938	5
169	Jan-1996	1123	957	7
170	Feb-1996	964	967	8
171	Mar-1996	1159	974	9
172	Apr-1996	1037	988	11
173	May-1996	1035	994	11
174	Jun-1996	1064	1002	12
175	Jul-1996	1083	1019	13
176	Aug-1996	962	1014	12
177	Sept-1996	922	1021	13
178	Oct-1996	915	1016	11
179	Nov-1996	866	1002	7
180	Dec-1996	907	1003	7

181	Jan-1997	1031	995	4
182	Feb-1997	895	990	2
183	Mar-1997	932	971	0
184	Apr-1997	931	962	-3
185	May-1997	867	948	-5
186	Jun-1997	875	932	-7
187	Jul-1997	820	910	-11
188	Aug-1997	824	899	-11
189	Sept-1997	696	880	-14
190	Oct-1997	878	877	-14
191	Nov-1997	573	852	-15
192	Dec-1997	763	840	-16
193	Jan-1998	697	813	-18
194	Feb-1998	679	795	-20
195	Mar-1998	848	788	-19
196	Apr-1998	735	771	-20
197	May-1998	602	749	-21
198	Jun-1998	655	731	-22
199	Jul-1998	648	717	-21
200	Aug-1998	574	696	-23
201	Sept-1998	553	684	-22
202	Oct-1998	605	661	-25
203	Nov-1998	551	659	-23
204	Dec-1998	619	647	-23
205	Jan-1999	559	636	-22
206	Feb-1999	573	627	-21
207	Mar-1999	623	608	-23
208	Apr-1999	553	593	-23
209	May-1999	414	577	-23
210	Jun-1999	501	564	-23
211	Jul-1999	459	549	-23
212	Aug-1999	456	539	-23
213	Sept-1999	419	528	-23
214	Oct-1999	489	518	-22
215	Nov-1999	469	511	-22
216	Dec-1999	447	497	-23
217	Jan-2000	608	501	-21
218	Feb-2000	474	493	-21

219	Mar-2000	494	482	-21
220	Apr-2000	462	474	-20
221	May-2000	499	481	-17
222	Jun-2000	473	479	-15
223	Jul-2000	381	473	-14
224	Aug-2000	489	475	-12
225	Sept-2000	395	473	-10
226	Oct-2000	434	469	-10
227	Nov-2000	384	462	-10
228	Dec-2000	379	456	-8
229	Jan-2001	470	445	-11
230	Feb-2001	403	439	-11
231	Mar-2001	508	440	-9
232	Apr-2001	481	441	-7
233	May-2001	480	440	-9
234	Jun-2001	480	440	-8
235	Jul-2001	475	448	-5
236	Aug-2001	505	450	-5
237	Sept-2001	374	448	-5
238	Oct-2001	517	455	-3
239	Nov-2001	501	464	1
240	Dec-2001	532	477	5
241	Jan-2002	604	488	10
242	Feb-2002	653	509	16
243	Mar-2002	553	513	17
244	Apr-2002	474	512	16
245	May-2002	527	516	17
246	Jun-2002	442	513	17
247	Jul-2002	458	511	14
248	Aug-2002	512	512	14
249	Sept-2002	378	513	14
250	Oct-2002	514	512	13
251	Nov-2002	410	505	9
252	Dec-2002	461	499	5
253	Jan-2003	488	489	0
254	Feb-2003	480	475	-7
255	Mar-2003	474	468	-9
256	Apr-2003	459	467	-9

257	May-2003	400	456	-12
258	Jun-2003	420	455	-11
259	Jul-2003	426	452	-12
260	Aug-2003	370	440	-14
261	Sept-2003	459	447	-13
262	Oct-2003	467	443	-14
263	Nov-2003	329	436	-14
264	Dec-2003	395	431	-14
265	Jan-2004	385	422	-14
266	Feb-2004	388	414	-13
267	Mar-2004	388	407	-13
268	Apr-2004	376	400	-14
269	May-2004	325	394	-14
270	Jun-2004	355	389	-15
271	Jul-2004	344	381	-16
272	Aug-2004	293	375	-15
273	Sep-2004	300	361	-19
274	Oct-2004	361	352	-20
275	Nov-2004	368	356	-18
276	Dec-2004	387	355	-18
277	Jan-2005	393	356	-16
278	Feb-2005	387	356	-14
279	Mar-2005	416	358	-12
280	Apr-2005	392	359	-10
281	May-2005	396	365	-7
282	Jun-2005	397	369	-5
283	Jul-2005	353	370	-3
284	Aug-2005	395	379	1
285	Sep-2005	472	393	9
286	Oct-2005	459	401	14
287	Nov-2005	417	405	14
288	Dec-2005	603	423	19
289	Jan-2006	600	441	24
290	Feb-2006	606	459	29
291	Mar-2006	700	483	35
292	Apr-2006	603	500	39
293	May-2006	746	529	45
294	Jun-2006	727	557	51

295	Jul-2006	790	593	60
296	Aug-2006	940	639	69
297	Sept-2006	1032	685	74
298	Oct-2006	1133	741	85
299				
300				
301				
302				
303				
304				
305				
306				
307				
308				
309				
310				
311				
312				
313				
314				
315				
316				
317				
318				
319				
320				
321				
322				
323				
324				

Source: San Diego County Recorders Office

Market Momentum Worksheet
Vital Sign #4 Foreclosure Sales (San Diego, CA): 1982-2006

Column A Month	Column B Month and Year	Column C Vital Sign Monthly Data	Column D 12-month Moving Average	Column E Vital Sign Momentum Reading
1	Jan-1982	190		
2	Feb-1982	179		
3	Mar-1982	251		
4	Apr-1982	223		
5	May-1982	206		
6	Jun-1982	260		
7	Jul-1982	238		
8	Aug-1982	268		
9	Sept-1982	287		
10	Oct-1982	366		
11	Nov-1982	309		
12	Dec-1982	306	257	
13	Jan-1983	283	265	
14	Feb-1983	302	275	
15	Mar-1983	339	282	
16	Apr-1983	338	292	
17	May-1983	343	303	
18	Jun-1983	357	311	
19	Jul-1983	357	321	
20	Aug-1983	423	334	
21	Sept-1983	334	338	
22	Oct-1983	321	334	
23	Nov-1983	306	334	
24	Dec-1983	368	339	32
25	Jan-1984	243	336	27
26	Feb-1984	301	335	22
27	Mar-1984	346	336	19
28	Apr-1984	304	333	14

29	May-1984	307	330	9
30	Jun-1984	257	322	4
31	Jul-1984	271	315	-2
32	Aug-1984	293	304	-9
33	Sept-1984	235	296	-12
34	Oct-1984	532	314	-6
35	Nov-1984	209	306	-9
36	Dec-1984	229	294	-13
37	Jan-1985	286	298	-11
38	Feb-1985	205	290	-14
39	Mar-1985	311	287	-15
40	Apr-1985	232	281	-16
41	May-1985	234	275	-17
42	Jun-1985	263	275	-15
43	Jul-1985	170	267	-15
44	Aug-1985	277	265	-13
45	Sept-1985	221	264	-11
46	Oct-1985	285	244	-22
47	Nov-1985	229	245	-20
48	Dec-1985	195	242	-18
49	Jan-1986	232	238	-20
50	Feb-1986	219	239	-17
51	Mar-1986	253	234	-18
52	Apr-1986	275	238	-15
53	May-1986	202	235	-14
54	Jun-1986	273	236	-14
55	Jul-1986	188	237	-11
56	Aug-1986	220	233	-12
57	Sept-1986	225	233	-12
58	Oct-1986	253	230	-5
59	Nov-1986	236	231	-6
60	Dec-1986	216	233	-4
61	Jan-1987	210	231	-3
62	Feb-1987	215	231	-4
63	Mar-1987	206	227	-3
64	Apr-1987	203	221	-7
65	May-1987	202	221	-6
66	Jun-1987	219	216	-8

67	Jul-1987	187	216	-9
68	Aug-1987	195	214	-8
69	Sept-1987	195	211	-9
70	Oct-1987	183	206	-11
71	Nov-1987	197	202	-12
72	Dec-1987	179	199	-14
73	Jan-1988	156	195	-16
74	Feb-1988	196	193	-16
75	Mar-1988	209	193	-15
76	Apr-1988	162	190	-14
77	May-1988	133	184	-16
78	Jun-1988	176	181	-16
79	Jul-1988	144	177	-18
80	Aug-1988	155	174	-19
81	Sept-1988	135	169	-20
82	Oct-1988	121	164	-20
83	Nov-1988	123	157	-22
84	Dec-1988	141	154	-23
85	Jan-1989	110	150	-23
86	Feb-1989	116	144	-26
87	Mar-1989	102	135	-30
88	Apr-1989	121	131	-31
89	May-1989	109	129	-.30
90	Jun-1989	117	125	-31
91	Jul-1989	97	121	-32
92	Aug-1989	82	115	-34
93	Sept-1989	88	111	-34
94	Oct-1989	100	109	-33
95	Nov-1989	77	105	-33
96	Dec-1989	90	101	-35
97	Jan-1990	84	99	-34
98	Feb-1990	85	96	-33
99	Mar-1990	101	96	-29
100	Apr-1990	72	92	-30
101	May-1990	80	89	-31
102	Jun-1990	88	87	-30
103	Jul-1990	93	87	-28
104	Aug-1990	81	87	-24

105	Sept-1990	85	86	-22
106	Oct-1990	111	87	-20
107	Nov-1990	108	90	-15
108	Dec-1990	92	90	-11
109	Jan-1991	121	93	-6
110	Feb-1991	136	97	1
111	Mar-1991	128	100	4
112	Apr-1991	152	106	16
113	May-1991	182	115	28
114	Jun-1991	157	120	38
115	Jul-1991	144	125	44
116	Aug-1991	185	133	54
117	Sept-1991	189	142	65
118	Oct-1991	213	151	73
119	Nov-1991	186	157	75
120	Dec-1991	320	176	96
121	Jan-1992	310	192	106
122	Feb-1992	224	199	105
123	Mar-1992	291	213	114
124	Apr-1992	305	226	112
125	May-1992	281	234	104
126	Jun-1992	338	249	107
127	Jul-1992	335	265	112
128	Aug-1992	332	277	108
129	Sept-1992	414	296	108
130	Oct-1992	317	304	102
131	Nov-1992	315	315	101
132	Dec-1992	365	319	81
133	Jan-1993	385	325	70
134	Feb-1993	357	336	69
135	Mar-1993	412	346	63
136	Apr-1993	368	352	56
137	May-1993	369	359	54
138	Jun-1993	449	368	48
139	Jul-1993	448	378	43
140	Aug-1993	509	392	42
141	Sept-1993	421	393	33
142	Oct-1993	439	403	32

143	Nov-1993	424	412	31
144	Dec-1993	529	426	34
145	Jan-1994	511	436	34
146	Feb-1994	417	441	31
147	Mar-1994	536	452	30
148	Apr-1994	445	458	30
149	May-1994	452	465	30
150	Jun-1994	426	463	26
151	Jul-1994	420	461	22
152	Aug-1994	446	456	16
153	Sept-1994	460	459	17
154	Oct-1994	383	454	13
155	Nov-1994	416	453	10
156	Dec-1994	426	445	04
157	Jan-1995	445	439	01
158	Feb-1995	415	439	0
159	Mar-1995	500	436	-3
160	Apr-1995	419	434	-5
161	May-1995	428	432	-7
162	Jun-1995	461	435	-6
163	Jul-1995	420	435	-6
164	Aug-1995	465	437	-4
165	Sept-1995	438	435	-5
166	Oct-1995	410	437	-4
167	Nov-1995	437	439	-3
168	Dec-1995	429	439	-1
169	Jan-1996	523	445	1
170	Feb-1996	454	449	2
171	Mar-1996	501	449	3
172	Apr-1996	513	457	5
173	May-1996	512	464	7
174	Jun-1996	464	464	7
175	Jul-1996	589	478	10
176	Aug-1996	514	482	10
177	Sept-1996	476	485	12
178	Oct-1996	522	495	13
179	Nov-1996	437	495	13
180	Dec-1996	489	500	14

181	Jan-1997	550	502	13
182	Feb-1997	474	503	12
183	Mar-1997	479	502	12
184	Apr-1997	467	498	9
185	May-1997	396	488	5
186	Jun-1997	453	487	5
187	Jul-1997	472	477	0
188	Aug-1997	389	467	-3
189	Sept-1997	373	458	-6
190	Oct-1997	392	448	-9
191	Nov-1997	328	439	-11
192	Dec-1997	363	428	-14
193	Jan-1998	392	415	-17
194	Feb-1998	312	401	-20
195	Mar-1998	343	390	-22
196	Apr-1998	294	376	-25
197	May-1998	274	365	-25
198	Jun-1998	303	353	-28
199	Jul-1998	298	338	-29
200	Aug-1998	234	326	-30
201	Sept-1998	236	314	-31
202	Oct-1998	230	301	-33
203	Nov-1998	199	290	-34
204	Dec-1998	230	279	-35
205	Jan-1999	198	263	-37
206	Feb-1999	189	252	-37
207	Mar-1999	239	244	-38
208	Apr-1999	155	232	-38
209	May-1999	163	223	-39
210	Jun-1999	165	211	-40
211	Jul-1999	181	202	-40
212	Aug-1999	162	196	-40
213	Sept-1999	125	186	-41
214	Oct-1999	147	179	-40
215	Nov-1999	139	174	-40
216	Dec-1999	126	166	-41
217	Jan-2000	113	159	-40
218	Feb-2000	122	153	-39

219	Mar-2000	126	144	-41
220	Apr-2000	125	141	-39
221	May-2000	97	136	-39
222	Jun-2000	187	138	-35
223	Jul-2000	99	131	-35
224	Aug-2000	113	127	-35
225	Sept-2000	83	123	-34
226	Oct-2000	80	118	-35
227	Nov-2000	96	114	-35
228	Dec-2000	139	115	-31
229	Jan-2001	59	111	-30
230	Feb-2001	68	106	-31
231	Mar-2001	56	100	-30
232	Apr-2001	52	94	-33
233	May-2001	65	91	-33
234	Jun-2001	55	80	-42
235	Jul-2001	51	76	-42
236	Aug-2001	74	73	-42
237	Sept-2001	75	73	-41
238	Oct-2001	77	72	-39
239	Nov-2001	85	71	-37
240	Dec-2001	109	69	-40
241	Jan-2002	76	70	-36
242	Feb-2002	54	69	-35
243	Mar-2002	105	73	-27
244	Apr-2002	90	76	-19
245	May-2002	50	75	-18
246	Jun-2002	54	75	-7
247	Jul-2002	132	82	7
248	Aug-2002	54	80	9
249	Sept-2002	44	78	7
250	Oct-2002	68	77	6
251	Nov-2002	42	73	3
252	Dec-2002	139	76	10
253	Jan-2003	48	73	4
254	Feb-2003	24	71	3
255	Mar-2003	52	66	-9
256	Apr-2003	39	62	-19

257	May-2003	23	60	-20
258	Jun-2003	61	61	-19
259	Jul-2003	50	54	-34
260	Aug-2003	47	53	-34
261	Sept-2003	60	54	-30
262	Oct-2003	54	53	-31
263	Nov-2003	15	51	-30
264	Dec-2003	93	47	-38
265	Jan-2004	33	46	-37
266	Feb-2004	67	50	-30
267	Mar-2004	39	48	-27
268	Apr-2004	50	49	-21
269	May-2004	46	51	-14
270	Jun-2004	68	52	-14
271	Jul-2004	33	50	-6
272	Aug-2004	79	53	-5
273	Sep-2004	42	52	-5
274	Oct-2004	58	52	-3
275	Nov-2004	15	52	2
276	Dec-2004	23	46	-2
277	Jan-2005	41	47	2
278	Feb-2005	12	42	-15
279	Mar-2005	28	41	-15
280	Apr-2005	25	39	-21
281	May-2005	41	39	-24
282	Jun-2005	61	38	-26
283	Jul-2005	28	38	-25
284	Aug-2005	68	37	-31
285	Sep-2005	67	39	-25
286	Oct-2005	52	38	-26
287	Nov-2005	68	43	-17
288	Dec-2005	68	47	1
289	Jan-2006	62	48	3
290	Feb-2006	73	53	27
219	Mar-2006	106	60	45
220	Apr-2006	114	67	72
221	May-2006	134	75	94
222	Jun-2006	158	83	118

223	Jul-2006	190	97	156
224	Aug-2006	174	106	186
225	Sept-2006	197	116	199
226	Oct-2006	251	133	246
227				
228				
229				
230				
231				
232				
233				
234				
235				
236				
237				
238				
239				
240				
241				
242				
243				
244				
245				
246				
247				
248				
249				
250				
251				
252				

Source: San Diego County Recorders Office

Appendix

Market Momentum Worksheet
Vital Sign #5
Interest Rates (30-Year Fixed-Rate Mortgages): 1982-2006

Column A Month	Column B Month and Year	Column C Vital Sign Monthly Data (%)	Column D 12-month Moving Average (%)	Column E Vital Sign Momentum Reading
1	Jan-1982	17.40		
2	Feb-1982	17.60		
3	Mar-1982	17.16		
4	Apr-1982	16.89		
5	May-1982	16.68		
6	Jun-1982	16.70		
7	Jul-1982	16.82		
8	Aug-1982	16.27		
9	Sept-1982	15.43		
10	Oct-1982	14.61		
11	Nov-1982	13.83		
12	Dec-1982	13.62	16.08	
13	Jan-1983	13.25	15.74	
14	Feb-1983	13.04	15.36	
15	Mar-1983	12.80	15.00	
16	Apr-1983	12.78	14.65	
17	May-1983	12.63	14.32	
18	Jun-1983	12.87	14.00	
18	Jul-1983	13.42	13.71	
20	Aug-1983	13.81	13.51	
21	Sept-1983	13.73	13.37	
22	Oct-1983	13.54	13.28	
23	Nov-1983	13.44	13.24	
24	Dec-1983	13.42	13.23	-18
25	Jan-1984	13.37	13.24	-16
26	Feb-1984	13.23	13.25	-14
27	Mar-1984	13.39	13.30	-11
28	Apr-1984	13.65	13.38	-9

29	May-1984	13.94	13.48	-6
30	Jun-1984	14.42	13.61	-3
31	Jul-1984	14.67	13.72	0
32	Aug-1984	14.47	13.77	2
33	Sept-1984	14.35	13.82	3
34	Oct-1984	14.13	13.87	4
35	Nov-1984	13.64	13.89	5
36	Dec-1984	13.18	13.87	5
37	Jan-1985	13.08	13.85	5
38	Feb-1985	12.92	13.82	4
39	Mar-1985	13.17	13.80	4
40	Apr-1985	13.20	13.76	3
41	May-1985	12.91	13.68	1
42	Jun-1985	12.22	13.50	-1
43	Jul-1985	12.04	13.28	-3
44	Aug-1985	12.19	13.09	-5
45	Sept-1985	12.19	12.91	-7
46	Oct-1985	12.14	12.74	-8
47	Nov-1985	11.78	12.59	-9
48	Dec-1985	11.26	12.43	-10
49	Jan-1986	10.88	12.24	-12
50	Feb-1986	10.71	12.06	-13
51	Mar-1986	10.08	11.80	-15
52	Apr-1986	10.14	11.30	-17
53	May-1986	10.68	11.17	-17
54	Jun-1986	10.68	11.17	-17
55	Jul-1986	10.51	11.04	-17
56	Aug-1986	10.42	10.88	-17
57	Sept-1986	10.01	10.69	-17
58	Oct-1986	9.97	10.51	-17
59	Nov-1986	9.70	10.34	-18
60	Dec-1986	9.31	10.18	-18
61	Jan-1987	9.20	10.04	-18
62	Feb-1987	9.08	9.90	-18
63	Mar-1987	9.04	9.82	-17
64	Apr-1987	9.83	9.81	-15
65	May-1987	10.60	9.84	-13
66	Jun-1987	10.54	9.83	-12

67	Jul-1987	10.28	9.81	-11
68	Aug-1987	10.33	7.82	-10
69	Sept-1987	10.89	9.90	-7
70	Oct-1987	11.26	10.01	-5
71	Nov-1987	10.65	10.08	-2
72	Dec-1987	10.65	10.20	0
73	Jan-1988	10.43	10.30	3
74	Feb-1988	9.89	10.37	5
75	Mar-1988	9.93	10.44	6
76	Apr-1988	10.20	10.47	7
77	May-1988	10.45	10.46	6
78	Jun-1988	10.46	10.45	6
79	Jul-1988	10.43	10.46	7
80	Aug-1988	10.60	10.49	7
81	Sept-1988	10.48	10.45	6
82	Oct-1988	10.30	10.37	4
83	Nov-1988	10.37	10.35	3
84	Dec-1988	10.61	10.35	1
85	Jan-1989	10.73	10.37	1
86	Feb-1989	10.64	10.43	1
87	Mar-1989	11.03	10.53	1
88	Apr-1989	11.05	10.60	1
89	May-1989	10.77	10.62	2
90	Jun-1989	10.20	10.60	1
91	Jul-1989	9.88	10.56	1
92	Aug-1989	9.99	10.50	0
93	Sept-1989	10.13	10.48	0
94	Oct-1989	9.95	10.45	1
95	Nov-1989	9.77	10.40	0
96	Dec-1989	9.74	10.32	0
97	Jan-1990	9.90	10.25	-1
98	Feb-1990	10.20	10.22	-2
99	Mar-1990	10.27	10.15	-4
100	Apr-1990	10.37	10.10	-5
101	May-1990	10.48	10.07	-5
102	Jun-1990	10.16	10.07	-5
103	Jul-1990	10.04	10.08	-4
104	Aug-1990	10.10	10.09	-4

105	Sept-1990	10.17	10.10	-4
106	Oct-1990	10.18	10.12	-3
107	Nov-1990	10.01	10.14	-3
108	Dec-1990	9.67	10.13	-2
109	Jan-1991	9.64	10.11	-1
110	Feb-1991	9.37	10.04	-2
111	Mar-1991	9.50	9.97	-2
112	Apr-1991	9.49	9.90	-2
113	May-1991	9.47	9.82	-3
114	Jun-1991	9.62	9.77	-3
115	Jul-1991	9.58	9.73	-3
116	Aug-1991	9.24	9.66	-4
117	Sept-1991	9.01	9.57	-5
118	Oct-1991	8.86	9.46	-7
119	Nov-1991	8.71	9.35	-8
120	Dec-1991	8.50	9.25	-9
121	Jan-1992	8.43	9.15	-9
122	Feb-1992	8.76	9.10	-9
123	Mar-1992	8.93	9.05	-9
124	Apr-1992	8.85	9.00	-9
125	May-1992	8.67	8.93	-9
126	Jun-1992	8.51	8.84	-10
127	Jul-1992	8.13	8.72	-10
128	Aug-1992	7.98	8.61	-11
129	Sept-1992	7.92	8.52	-11
130	Oct-1992	8.09	8.46	-11
131	Nov-1992	8.31	8.42	-10
132	Dec-1992	8.22	8.40	-9
133	Jan-1993	8.02	8.37	-9
134	Feb-1993	7.68	8.28	-9
135	Mar-1993	7.50	8.16	-10
136	Apr-1993	7.47	8.04	-11
137	May-1993	7.47	7.94	-11
138	Jun-1993	7.42	7.85	-11
139	Jul-1993	7.21	7.77	-11
140	Aug-1993	7.11	7.70	-11
141	Sept-1993	6.92	7.62	-11
142	Oct-1993	6.83	7.51	-11

143	Nov-1993	7.16	7.42	-12
144	Dec-1993	7.17	7.33	-13
145	Jan-1994	7.06	7.25	-13
146	Feb-1994	7.15	7.21	-13
147	Mar-1994	7.68	7.22	-11
148	Apr-1994	8.32	7.29	-9
149	May-1994	8.60	7.39	-7
150	Jun-1994	8.40	7.47	-5
151	Jul-1994	8.61	7.58	-2
152	Aug-1994	8.52	7.70	0
153	Sept-1994	8.64	7.85	3
154	Oct-1994	8.93	8.02	7
155	Nov-1994	9.17	8.19	10
156	Dec-1994	9.20	8.36	14
157	Jan-1995	9.15	8.53	18
158	Feb-1995	8.83	8.67	20
159	Mar-1995	8.46	8.74	21
160	Apr-1995	8.32	8.74	20
161	May-1995	7.96	8.68	18
162	Jun-1995	7.57	8.61	15
163	Jul-1995	7.61	8.53	12
164	Aug-1995	7.86	8.48	10
165	Sept-1995	7.64	8.39	7
166	Oct-1995	7.48	8.27	3
167	Nov-1995	7.38	8.12	-1
168	Dec-1995	7.20	7.96	-5
169	Jan-1996	7.03	7.78	-9
170	Feb-1996	7.08	7.63	-12
171	Mar-1996	7.63	7.56	-13
172	Apr-1996	7.92	7.53	-14
173	May-1996	8.07	7.54	-13
174	Jun-1996	8.32	7.60	-12
175	Jul-1996	8.25	7.66	-10
176	Aug-1996	8.00	6.67	-10
177	Sept-1996	8.23	7.72	-8
178	Oct-1996	7.92	7.75	-6
179	Nov-1996	7.62	7.77	-4
180	Dec-1996	7.60	7.81	-2

181	Jan-1997	7.82	7.87	1
182	Feb-1997	7.65	7.92	4
183	Mar-1997	7.90	7.94	5
184	Apr-1997	8.14	7.96	6
185	May-1997	7.94	7.95	5
186	Jun-1997	7.69	7.90	4
187	Jul-1997	7.50	7.83	2
188	Aug-1997	7.48	7.79	2
189	Sept-1997	7.43	7.72	0
190	Oct-1997	7.29	7.67	-1
191	Nov-1997	7.21	7.64	-2
192	Dec-1997	7.10	7.60	-3
193	Jan-1998	6.99	7.53	-4
194	Feb-1998	7.40	7.48	-6
195	Mar-1998	7.13	7.41	-7
196	Apr-1998	7.14	7.33	-8
197	May-1998	7.14	7.26	-9
198	Jun-1998	7.00	7.20	-9
199	Jul-1998	6.95	7.16	-9
200	Aug-1998	6.92	7.11	-9
201	Sept-1998	6.72	7.05	-9
202	Oct-1998	6.71	7.00	-9
203	Nov-1998	6.87	6.98	-9
204	Dec-1998	6.72	6.94	-9
205	Jan-1999	6.79	6.93	-8
206	Feb-1999	6.81	6.91	-8
207	Mar-1999	7.04	6.90	-7
208	Apr-1999	6.92	6.88	-6
209	May-1999	7.15	6.88	-5
210	Jun-1999	7.55	6.93	-4
211	Jul-1999	7.63	6.99	-2
212	Aug-1999	7.94	7.07	-1
213	Sept-1999	7.82	7.16	2
214	Oct-1999	7.85	7.26	4
215	Nov-1999	7.74	7.33	5
216	Dec-1999	7.91	7.43	7
217	Jan-2000	8.21	7.55	9
218	Feb-2000	8.33	7.67	11

219	Mar-2000	8.24	7.77	13
220	Apr-2000	8.15	7.88	14
221	May-2000	8.52	7.99	16
222	Jun-2000	8.29	8.05	16
223	Jul-2000	8.15	8.10	16
224	Aug-2000	8.03	8.10	15
225	Sept-2000	7.91	8.11	13
226	Oct-2000	7.80	8.11	12
227	Nov-2000	7.75	8.11	11
228	Dec-2000	7.38	8.06	9
229	Jan-2001	7.03	7.97	6
230	Feb-2001	7.05	7.86	2
231	Mar-2001	6.95	7.75	0
232	Apr-2001	7.07	7.66	-3
233	May-2001	7.14	7.55	-6
234	Jun-2001	7.16	7.45	-7
235	Jul-2001	7.13	7.37	-9
236	Aug-2001	6.95	7.28	-10
237	Sept-2001	6.82	7.19	-11
238	Oct-2001	6.62	7.09	-13
239	Nov-2001	6.66	7.00	-14
240	Dec-2001	7.07	6.97	-14
241	Jan-2002	7.00	6.97	-13
242	Feb-2002	6.89	6.96	-11
243	Mar-2002	7.01	6.96	-10
244	Apr-2002	6.99	6.95	-9
245	May-2002	6.81	6.93	-8
246	Jun-2002	6.65	6.88	-8
247	Jul-2002	6.49	6.83	-7
248	Aug-2002	6.29	6.78	-7
249	Sept-2002	6.09	6.71	-7
250	Oct-2002	6.11	6.67	-6
251	Nov-2002	6.07	6.62	-5
252	Dec-2002	6.05	6.54	-6
253	Jan-2003	5.92	6.45	-7
254	Feb-2003	5.84	6.36	-9
255	Mar-2003	5.75	6.26	-10
256	Apr-2003	5.81	6.16	-11

257	May-2003	5.49	6.05	-13
258	Jun-2003	5.23	5.93	-14
259	Jul-2003	5.63	5.86	-14
260	Aug-2003	6.24	5.85	-14
261	Sept-2003	6.15	5.86	-13
262	Oct-2003	5.95	5.84	-12
263	Nov-2003	5.93	5.83	-12
264	Dec-2003	5.88	5.82	-11
265	Jan-2004	5.74	5.80	-10
266	Feb-2004	5.64	5.79	-9
267	Mar-2004	5.45	5.76	-8
268	Apr-2004	5.83	5.76	-6
269	May-2004	6.27	5.83	-4
270	Jun-2004	6.29	5.92	0
271	Jul-2004	6.06	5.95	2
272	Aug-2004	5.87	5.92	1
273	Sep-2004	5.75	5.89	1
274	Oct-2004	5.72	5.87	0
275	Nov-2004	5.73	5.85	0
276	Dec-2004	5.75	5.84	0
277	Jan-2005	5.71	5.84	1
278	Feb-2005	5.63	5.84	1
279	Mar-2005	5.93	5.88	2
280	Apr-2005	5.86	5.88	2
281	May-2005	5.72	5.84	0
282	Jun-2005	5.58	5.78	-2
283	Jul-2005	5.70	5.75	-3
284	Aug-2005	5.82	5.74	-3
285	Sep-2005	5.77	5.74	-2
286	Oct-2005	6.07	5.77	-2
287	Nov-2005	6.33	5.82	0
288	Dec-2005	6.27	5.87	0
217	Jan-2006	6.15	5.90	1
218	Feb-2006	6.25	5.95	2
219	Mar-2006	6.32	5.99	2
220	Apr-2006	6.51	6.04	3
221	May-2006	6.60	6.11	5
222	Jun-2006	6.68	6.21	7

223	Jul-2006	6.76	6.29	10
224	Aug-2006	6.52	6.35	11
225	Sept-2006	6.40	6.41	12
226	Oct-2006	6.36	6.43	11
227				
228				
229				
230				
231				
232				
233				
234				
235				
236				
237				
238				
239				
240				
241				
242				
243				
244				
245				
246				
247				
248				
249				
250				
251				
252				

Source: Federal Reserve Bank of St. Louis (www.research.stlouisfed.org/)

About the Author

Robert Campbell has been living and breathing real estate from the time he learned how to walk. The son of a successful San Diego homebuilder, he spent many hours as a youngster tagging along with his dad to the lumberyard, and later worked on his father's construction sites to help pay his way through college. But Robert quickly learned that there was far more to real estate than dirt, concrete, lumber and building materials. Early on, he learned that real estate markets are a lot like roller-coaster rides, where spectacular climbs are as common as spectacular falls.

Robert graduated from UCLA and started investing in real estate at age 24, borrowing $14,000 from his parents for the down payment on a 6-unit apartment house. After doing some cosmetic repairs and raising the rents, he sold the property for an $11,000 profit one year later. He was hooked.

Since then, Robert Campbell has had a multifaceted 30-year real estate career that includes:

- As a real estate investor, he has bought and sold over 40 rental properties.

- As a real estate developer, he has built over 50 homes and apartment units.

- As a California real estate broker (licensed in 1976), he has handled the sales and mortgage financing for hundreds of clients.

- As a real estate advisor, he publishes the only timing advisory for Southern California real estate investors.

Information on "The Campbell Real Estate Timing Letter" can be found at www.CaliforniaRealEstateTiming.com.

As a university lecturer, he has given guest presentations at the University of San Diego, where Robert's book *Timing the San Diego Real Estate Market* has been used in classes on real estate investment.

A seasoned veteran of both good and bad real estate cycles, Robert Campbell has experienced many more successes than losses. Ironically, it was his biggest real estate "mistake" that inspired him to write this book.

Because Robert believes that "avoiding disaster" is one of the true secrets for achieving lasting, long-term prosperity — and because of his hard-won experiences, market observations, education, and analytical expertise–he has created *The Campbell Method* for tracking trends to buy and sell. This revolutionary approach to timing the real estate market not only provides you with the tools to survive the real estate roller-coaster ride, but it also presents a clearly defined method for achieving maximum profits.

Mr. Campbell earned a BA in Economics from the University of California at Los Angeles in 1969 and an M.B.A. in Real Estate Finance from San Diego State University in 1974.

You can reach Robert Campbell by phone: 858-481-3235 or by email at Robert@RealEstateTiming.com.

Your Chance To Be Famous!

If you liked *Timing the San Diego Real Estate Market*, write me a testimonial. A selection of testimonials will be included in the future editions of this book and will also be added to my website at RealEstateTiming.com.

Please send to Robert M. Campbell, 3235 Del Mar Heights Road #634, San Diego, California 92130 or email to: Robert@RealEstateTiming.com.

Important note: when you send a testimonial, it is understood that you are giving me permission to use it for marketing purposes.

Want a Free Copy of this Book?

Do you have any insights, comments, or personal stories to share that will improve this book?

If so, please send them to me. If your submittal is included in the next edition of *Timing the San Diego Real Estate Market*, a free copy will be sent to you.

$pread the Word and $ave 20%

Recommend this book to your friends and they can buy it at a 20% DISCOUNT.

Simply fill out the "Spread the Word" order form, send it to your friend or colleague who might be interested in this book, and . . . Voila! . . . They can buy it for $19.95 (not the regular price of $24.95).

Spread the Word

Please fax or pass this on to friends and colleagues who could profit from this book.

To _____
From _____

I have just read the book *Timing the San Diego Real Estate Market* by Robert Campbell. This is what I think of it:

_____
_____
_____
_____

If you use this order form I sent you, you will receive a 20% discount: $19.95 per copy instead of $24.95. Enjoy the book.

"Brilliant, absolutely brilliant. If you want to make more money in real estate, follow The Campbell Method for the best times to buy and sell. I give this book my highest rating. Five stars!"

— Robert G. Allen, best selling author of *Nothing Down*, *Creating Wealth*, and *Multiple Streams of Income*.

Order Form

Yes, I want ___ copies of *Timing the San Diego Real Estate Market* @ $19.95 each + $5.00 shipping and handling. ($24.95 total per book). California residents add 7.75% ($1.55) for sales tax.

My check for $_____ is enclosed.

Name: _____
Company: _____
Address: _____
City: _____ State: _____ Zip: _____
Phone: (_____) _____ Email: _____

Make checks payable to Robert Campbell

Mail to: Robert M. Campbell, 3525 Del Mar Heights Road, #634, San Diego, CA 92130 (858) 481-3235

Market Momentum Charting **Software**

Do you want a fast, accurate and easy way to calculate the market momentum readings for the Vital Sign indicators . . . and then automatically create Vital Sign charts just like those shown in this book?

If so, simply fill out this order form, enclose a check for $29.95 + $5.00 shipping and handling ($34.95 total) and mail it to Robert M. Campbell.

Before you order, please note this: To run this *Market Momentum Charting* software, you need to have (1) Microsoft Excel (2000 or XP is best) and (2) Windows 2000, ME or XP installed on your computer.

Even if you are a computer dummy — and don't know a lot about Microsoft Excel — don't worry. *Market Momentum Charting* is incredibly simple to use. All you have to do is:

1) Put the disk into the CD holder of your computer.

2) Wait for the *Market Momentum Charting* worksheet to appear on your computer screen (this takes about five seconds).

3) Type in the dates and the Vital Sign data where indicated (24 months of data is required before you can create a chart — see Chapter 6)

4) Voila! You will instantly be looking at a Vital Sign chart.

Order Form for Market Momentum Charting Software

Name: _____

Company: _____

Address: _____

City: _____ State: ___ Zip: _____

Phone: (_____) _____

Email: _____

To order, mail this order form and a check for $34.95 (payable to Robert Campbell) to:

>Robert M. Campbell
>3525 Del Mar Heights Road, #634
>San Diego, CA 92130
>(858) 481-3235

Printed in the United States
76214LV00003B/13-108